William Lowes Rushton

Shakespeare's Euphuism

William Lowes Rushton

Shakespeare's Euphuism

ISBN/EAN: 9783337063719

Printed in Europe, USA, Canada, Australia, Japan

Cover: Foto ©Thomas Meinert / pixelio.de

More available books at **www.hansebooks.com**

SHAKESPEARE'S EUPHUISM.

BY

WILLIAM LOWES RUSHTON,

OF GRAY'S INN, BARRISTER-AT-LAW:

Corresponding Member of the Berlin Society for the Study of Modern Languages,
Author of 'Shakespeare a Lawyer,' 'Shakespeare's Legal Maxims,'
'Shakespeare illustrated by Old Authors,' 'Shakespeare
illustrated by the Lex Scripta,' 'Shakespeare's
Testamentary Language,' &c.

LONDON:
LONGMANS, GREEN, AND CO.
LIVERPOOL: ADAM HOLDEN, CHURCH STREET.
1871.

NOTICE.

I HAVE AGAIN tried to give many illustrations in a small space; therefore, when the extracts themselves explain the passages selected, I have made no comment. I have seen in various editions of Shakespeare a few quotations from the 'Euphues' of Lyly, but I am not aware that the commentators have made any of these illustrations.

Ullet Lane, Liverpool:
April, 1871.

SHAKESPEARE'S EUPHUISM.

> And still they gazed, and still the wonder grew
> That one small head could carry all he knew.
> *Goldsmith.*

THE Euphues of Lyly was published before Shakespeare began to write for the stage. It is said that 'all the ladies of the time were Lyly's scholars, she who spoke not Euphuism being as little regarded at Court as if she could not speak French,' and that 'his invention was so curiously strung that Elizabeth's Court held his notes in admiration.' It is evident that Shakespeare was very familiar with this book, wherein I see the origin of many of the famous passages in his works. Shakespeare and Lyly have often the same thoughts, use the same language and phrases, and play upon the same words.

Pan. Troilus! why, he esteems her no more than
I esteem an addle egg.
Cres. If you love an *addle egg* as well as you love
an *idle head*, you would eat chickens i' the shell.
Troilus and Cressida, Act i. Scene 2.

Yet may I of all the rest most condempne *Oxford* of vnkindnesse, of vice I cannot, who seemed to weane mee before she brought mee forth, and to giue mee boanes to gnawe, before I could get the teate to sucke. Wherein she played the nice mother in sending me into the Countrie to nurse, where I tyred at a drie breast three yeares, and was at the last inforced to weane my selfe. But it was destinie, for if I had not ben gathered from the tree in the bud, I should being blowen haue prooued a blast, and as good it is to be an *addle egge*, as an *idle bird*.

Tra. Mi perdonato, gentle master mine,
I am in all affected as yourself;
Glad that you thus continue your resolve
To suck the sweets of sweet philosophy.
Only, good master, while we do admire
This virtue and this moral discipline,
Let's be no *stoics* nor no *stocks*, I pray;
Or so devote to Aristotle's checks
As Ovid be an outcast quite abjured.
Taming the Shrew, Act i. Scene 1.

But so many men so many mindes, that may seeme

in your eye odious, which in an others eye may be gracious. *Aristippus* a Philosopher, yet who more courtly? *Diogenes* a Philosopher, yet who more carterly? Who more popular than *Plato* retayning alwayes good company? Who more enuious then *Tymon*, denouncing all humaine societie? Who so seuere as the *Stoickes*, which lyke *stocks* were moued with no melodie?

. . . .

Is it not the pray that enticeth the theefe to rifle? Is it not the pleasaunt bayte that causeth the fleetest fish to byte? Is it not a by worde amongst vs, that gold maketh an honest man an ill man? Did *Philautus* accompt *Euphues* too simple to decypher beautie, or superstitious not to desire it? Did he deeme him a saint in reiecting fancy, or a sot in not discerning it? Thought he him a *Stoycke*, that he woulde not be moued, or a *stocke* that he could not?

———————

Boyet. Who is the suitor? who is the suitor?
Ros.   Shall I teach you to know?
Boyet. Ay, my continent of beauty.
Ros.   Why, she that bears the *bow.*
        Love's Labour's Lost, Act iv. Scene 1.

There was a Lady in *Spaine,* who after the disease of hir Father hadde three sutors, (and yet neuer a good Archer) the one excelled in all giftes of the bodye, in-somuch that there could be nothing added to his perfection, and so armed in all poyntes, as his very lookes were able to pearce the heart of any Ladie, especially of such a one, as seemed hir selfe to haue no lesse beauty, than she had personage.

Lyly plays upon the word suitor by connecting it with the word archer, and Shakespeare by connecting it with the word bow.

King. *Most subject is the fattest soil to weeds:*
And he, the noble image of my youth,
Is overspread with them: therefore my grief
Stretches itself beyond the hour of death.
    2 *Henry IV.*, Act iv. Scene 4.

Doth not common experience make this common vnto vs that *the fattest ground bringeth foorth nothing but weedes* if it be not well tilled? That the sharpest wit enclyneth onely to wickedness, if it be not exercised?

King. O wretched state! O bosom black as death!
O limed soul, that struggling to be free,
Art more engaged!
    Hamlet, Act iii. Scene 3.

He that seeketh the depth of knowledge: is as it were in a *Laborinth,* in the which ye farther he goeth, the farther he is from the end: or like ye *bird in the limebush, which the more she striueth to get out, ye faster she sticketh in.*

Par. This is hard and undeserved measure, my lord.

Laf. Go to, sir: you were beaten in Italy for picking a kernel out of a pomegranate; you are a vagabond and no true traveller: you are more saucy with lords and honourable personages than the commission of your birth and virtue gives you heraldry.

All's Well that Ends Well, Act ii. Scene 3.

This letter beeing coyned, hee studyed how hee myght conueie it, knowing it to be no lesse perrilous to trust those hee knewe not in so weightye a case, then dyffycult for him-selfe to haue opportunitie to delyuer it in so suspitious a company: At the last taking out of his closette a fayre *Pomegranet*, and *pullyng all the kernelles out of it*, hee wrapped his Letter in it, closing the toppe of it finely, that it could not be perceyued, whether nature agayne hadde knitte it of purpose to further him, or his arte had ouercome nature's cunning. This pomegranet hee tooke, beeing him-selfe both messenger of his letter, and the mayster, and insinuating him-selfe into the companie of the Gentlewomen, among whom was also *Camilla*, he was welcommed as well for that he had beene long tyme absent, as for that hee was at all tymes pleasaunt, much good communication there was touching manye matters, which heere to insert were neyther conuenient, seeing it doth not concern the Hystorie, nor expedient, seeing it is nothing to the delyuerie of *Philautus* Letter.

Lafeu may mean that Parolles was punished for sending a letter in a pomegranate in this secret manner.

[*The Fourth Knight passes over.*
Sim. What is the fourth?
Thai. A burning *torch* that's *turned upside down*; The word, ' *Quod me alit, me extinguit.*'
Sim. Which shows that beauty hath his power and will.
Which can as well inflame as it can kill.
Pericles, Act ii. Scene 1.

Is this the nature of a Father to deceiue his sonne, or the part of crabbed age, to delude credulous youth? Is the death bedde which ought to bee the ende of deuotion, become the beginning of deceipt? Ah *Cassander*, friend I can-not terme thee, seeing thee so vnkinde: and father I will not call thee, whome I finde so vnnaturall.

Who so shall heare of this vngratefulnesse, will rather lament thy dealyng than thy death; and maruel yat a man affected outwardly with such great grauitie, should inwardly be infected with so great guile. Shall I then shew the ductie of a childe, when thou hast forgotten the Nature of a Father? No, no, for as the *Torch tourned downewarde, is extinguished with the selfe same waxe which was the cause of his lyght:* so Nature tourned to vnkindenesse, is quenched by those meanes it shoulde be kindeled, leauing no braunch of loue, where it founde no roote of humanitie.

Iago. Virtue! a fig! 'tis in ourselves that we are thus or thus. Our bodies are our gardens, to the which our wills are gardeners: so that if we will plant nettles, or sow lettuce, set *hyssop* and weed up *thyme*, supply it with one gender of herbs, or distract it with many, either to have it sterile with idleness, or manured with industry, why, the power and corrigible authority of this lies in our wills.
Othello, Act i. Scene 3.

King. But to the place where it standeth north-north-east and by east from the west corner of thy *curious-knotted* garden.
Love's Labour's Lost, Act i. Scene 1.

Serv. Why should we in the compass of a pale
Keep law and form and due proportion,
Showing, as in a model, our firm estate,
When our sea-walled garden, the whole land,
Is full of weeds, her fairest flowers choked up,
Her fruit-trees all unpruned, her hedges ruin'd,
Her *knots* disorder'd and her wholesome herbs
Swarming with caterpillars?
Richard II., Act iv. Scene 4.

They might also haue taken example of the wise

husbandmen, who in their fattest and most fertil ground sow Hempe before Wheat, a graine that dryeth vp the superfluous moysture, and maketh the soyle more apt for corne: Or of good Gardeiners who in their *curious knots* mixe *Hisoppe with Time* as ayders the one to the growth of the other, the one being drye, the other moyst: Or of cunning Painters, who for the whitest worke cast the blackest ground, to make ye picture more amiable. If therefore thy Father had bene as wise an husbandman as he was a fortunate husbande, or thy Mother as good a huswife as she was a happy wife, if they had bene both as good Gardeiners to keepe their *knotte*, as they were grafters to bring forth such fruit, or as cunning Painters, as they wer happy parents, no doubt they had sowed Hempe before Wheat, that is, discipline before affection, they had set *Hisoppe with Time*, that is, manners with witte, the one to ayde the other, and to make thy dexteritie more, they had cast a blacke grounde for their white worke, that is, they hadde mixed threates with faire lookes. But things past, are past calling againe: it is too late to shutte the stable doore when the steede is stolne. The *Troyans* repented too late when their towne was spoyled: Yet the remembraunce of thy former follyes, might breede in thee a remorce of conscience, and bee a remedie against farther concupiscence. But now to thy present time.

Shakespeare speaks of a *curious-knotted*

garden, and Lyly of good gardeners who in their *curious knots* mix hyssop with thyme.

Laer. To his good friends thus wide I'll ope my
    arms;
And like the kind *life-rendering pelican*
Repast them with my blood.
                Hamlet, Act iv. Scene 5.

It fareth with me *Psellus* as with the *Austrich*, who pricketh none but hir selfe, which causeth hir to runne when she would rest: or as it doth with *the Pelicane, who stricketh bloud out of hir owne bodye to do others good.*

Vio. I left no ring with her: what means this
    lady?
Fortune forbid my outside have not charmed her!
She made good view of me: indeed, so much
That sure methought *her eyes had lost her tongue*,
For she did speak in starts distractedly.
             Twelfth Night, Act ii. Scene 2.

But this I admonish you, that as your owne bewties make you not couetous of your almes towardes true louers, so other mens flatterie make you not prodigall of your honours towardes dissemblers. Let not them that speake fairest be beleeued soonest, for *true loue lacketh a tongue, and is tryed by the eyes,* whiche in a hearte that meaneth well, are as farre from wanton glaunces, as the minde is from idle thoughts.

Davy. Doth the man of war stay all night, sir?
Shal. Yea, Davy. I will use him well: *a friend i' the court is better than a penny in purse.*
2 *Henry IV.*, Act v. Scene 1.

Thou sayest I am much wished for, that many fayre promises are made to mee: Truly *Philautus* I know that *a friende in the court is better then a penney in the purse,* but yet I haue heard that suche a friend cannot be gotten in the court without pence.

Fal. I have writ me here a letter to her; and here another to Page's wife, who even now gave me good eyes too, examined my parts with most judicious œillades: sometimes the beam of her view gilded my foot, sometimes my portly belly.
Pist. Then did the sun on dunghill shine.
Merry Wives, Act i. Scene 2.

No, no! it is the disposition of the thought, that altereth the nature of the thing. *The Sunne shineth vpon the dounghil,* and is not corrupted: the Diamond lyeth in the fire, and is not consumed: the Christall toucheth the Toade and is not poysoned: the birde *Trochilus* lyueth by the mouth of the

Crocodile and is not spoyled : a perfect wit is neuer bewitched with leaudenesse, neither entised with lasciuiousnesse.

Caius. I pray you, bear vitness that me have stay six or seven, two, tree hours for him, and he is no come.

Shal. He is the wiser man, master doctor: he is a curer of souls, and you a curer of bodies; if you should fight, you *go against the hair* of your professions.
Merry Wives of Windsor, Act ii. Scene 3.

Oh my good *Euphues*, I haue neither the power to forsake mine owne *Camilla*, nor the heart to deny thy counsaile, it is easie to fall into a Nette, but hard to get out. Notwithstanding I will *goe against the haire* in all things, so I may please thee in anye thing, O my *Camilla*.

King. To bear all smooth and even,
This sudden sending him away must seem
Deliberate pause : *diseases desperate grown
By desperate appliances are relieved,*
Or not at all.
Hamlet, Act iv. Scene 3.

Now if thy cunning be answerable to thy good will, practise some pleasant conceipt vpon thy poore patient: one dram of *Ouids* art, some of *Tibullis* drugs, one of *Propertius* pilles, which may cause me either to purge my new disease, or recouer my hoped desire. But I feare me wher so straunge a sicknesse is to be recured of so vnskilfull a Phisition, that either thou wilt be to bold to practise, or my body too weake to purge. But seeing *a desperate disease is to be committed to a desperate Doctor*, I will follow thy counsel, and become thy cure, desiring thee to be as wise in ministring thy Phisick, as I haue bene willing to putte my lyfe into thy handes.

Adr. Ah, but I think him better than I say,
And yet would herein others' eyes were worse.
Far from her nest the lapwing cries away :
My heart prays for him, though my tongue do curse. *Comedy of Errors*, Act iv. Scene 2.

I haue brought into the worlde two children, of the first I was deliuered before my friendes thought mee conceiued, of the second I went a whole yeare big, and yet when euerye one thought me ready to lye downe, I did then quicken: But good huswiues shall make my excuse, who know that Hens do not lay egges when they clucke, but when they cackle, nor men set forth bookes when they promise, but when they performe. And in this I resemble the *Lappwing*, who fearing hir young ones to be destroyed by passengers, *flyeth with a false cry farre from their nestes*, making those that looke for them seeke where they are not.

Antony. O this false soul of Egypt! this grave charm—
Whose eye beck'd forth my wars, and call'd them home;
Whose bosom was my crownlet, my chief end,—
Like a right *gipsy*, hath, *at fast and loose*,
Beguiled me to the very heart of loss.
          Antony and Cleopatra, Act iv. Scene 12.

A wit sayest thou with-out loue, is lyke an Egge with-out salte, and a Courtier voyde of affection, like salt without sauour. Then as one pleasing thy selfe in thine owne humour, or playing with others for thine owne pleasure, thou rollest all thy wits to sifte Loue from Lust, as the Baker doth the branne from his flower, bringing in *Venus* with a Torteyse vnder hir foote, as slowe to harmes: hir Chariot drawen with white Swannes, as the cognisance of *Vesta*, hir birds to be Pigeons, noting pietie: with as many inuentions to make *Venus* currant, as the Ladies vse slights in *Italy* to make themselues counterfaite. Thus with the *Aegyptian thou playest fast or loose*, so that there is nothing more certeine, then that thou wilt loue, and nothing more vncerteine then when, tourning at one time thy tayle to the winde, with the Hedge-hogge, and thy nose in the winde, with the Weather-cocke, in one gale both hoysing sayle and weighing Anker, with one breath, making an Alarme and a Parly, discharging in the same instaunt, both a Bullet and a *false fire*.

Hamlet. What! frighted with *false fire!*
          Act iii. Scene 2.

Bed. Hung be the heavens with black, yield day
   to night!
Comets, importing change of times and states,
Brandish your crystal tresses in the sky,
And with them scourge the bad revolting stars
That have consented unto Henry's death!
            1 *Henry VI.*, Act i. Scene 1.

Cleanthes alleadged foure causes, which might induce man to acknowledge a God, the first by the foreseeing of things to come, the second by the infinite commodities which we daily reape, as by the temperature of the ayre, the fatnesse of the earth, the fruitefulnesse of trees, plants, and hearbes, the aboundaunce of all things that maye either serue for the necessitie of many, or the superfluitie of a few, the thirde by the terror that the minde of man is stroken into, by lyghtenings, thunderings, tempests, hayles, snowe, earthquakes, pestilence, by the straunge and terrible sights which cause vs to tremble, as the rayning of blond, the fierie impressions in the Element, the ouerflowing of floudes in the earth, the prodigious shapes and vnnaturall formes of men, of beastes, of birdes, of fishes, of all creatures, the appearing of blasing *Comettes, which euer prognosticate some straunge mutation*, the sight of two Sunnes which happened in the Consulshippe of *Tuditanus* and *Aquilius*, with these things mortall men being afrighted, are inforced to acknowledge an immortal and omnipotent god. The fourth by the equalytie in mouing in the heuen, the course of the Sunne, the order of the stars, the beautifulnesse of the Element, ye sight wheroff might sufficiently induce vs to beleeue they proceede not by chaunce, by nature, or destenie, but by the eternal and diuine purpose of some omnipotent Deitie. Heereoff it came that when the Philosophers could giue no reason by Nature, they would say there is one aboue Nature, an other would call him the first mouer, an other the ayder of Nature, and so foorth.

Brutus. What you have said
I will consider; what you have to say
I will with patience hear, and find a time
Both meet to hear and answer such high things.
Till then, my noble friend, *chew upon this*:
Brutus had rather be a villager
Than to repute himself a son of Rome
Under these hard conditions as this time
Is like to lay upon us.
Julius Cæsar, Act i. Scene 2.

Philautus dispatching a messenger with this letter speadely to *Euphues,* went into the fields to walk ther, either to digest his choler, or *chew vpon* his melancholy.

Well *Psellus,* thou hast wrought that in me, which thou wishest, for if the baites that are layde for beautie be so ridiculous, I thinke it of as great effect in loue, to vse a Plaister as a Potion.

I now vtterly dissent from those that imagine Magicke to be the meanes, and consent with thee, that thinkest letters to be, which I will vse, and howe I speede I will tell thee, in the meane season pardon me, if I vse no longer aunswere, for well you know, that he that hath the fit of an Ague vpon him, hath no lust to talke but to tumble, and Loue pinching me I haue more desire to *chew vpon* melancholy, then to dispute vpon Magicke, but heereafter I will make repaire vnto you, and what I now giue you in thankes, I will then requite with amends.

Thaisa. My wedded lord, I ne'er shall see again,
A vestal livery will I take me to,
And never more have joy.
 Cer. Madam, if this you purpose as ye speak,
Diana's temple is not distant far,
Where you may abide till *your date expire.*
     Pericles, Act iii. Scene 4.

I haue not yet forgotten the inuectiue (I can no otherwyse terme it) which thou madest against beauty, sayinge, it was a deceitful bayte with a deadly hooke, and a sweet poyson in a paynted pot. Canst thou then be so vnwise to swallowe the bayte which will breede thy bane? To swill the drinke that will *expyre thy date?* To desire the wight that will worke thy death? But it may be that with the Scorpion thou canst feede on the earth, or with the Quayle and Roebucke, be fat with poyson: or with beautye liue in all brauerye.

Iago. You or any man living may be drunk at a time, man. I'll tell you what you shall do. Our general's wife is now the general: I may say so in this respect, for that he hath devoted and given up himself to the contemplation, mark, and denotement of her parts and graces: confess yourself freely to her; importune her help to put you in your place again: she is of so free, so kind, so apt, so blessed a disposition, she holds it a vice in her goodness not to do more than she is requested: *this broken joint between you and her husband entreat her to splinter; and, my fortunes against any lay worth naming, this crack of your love shall grow stronger than it was before.*
Othello, Act ii. Scene 3.

Yes, yes, *Lucilla*, well doth he knowe that the glasse once crased, will with the least clappe be cracked, that the cloth which stayneth with milke, will soone loose his coulour with Vineger: that the Eagles wing will wast the feather as well of the *Phœnix*, as of the Pheasaunt: that she that hath beene faithlesse to one, will neuer be faithfull to any. But can *Euphues* conuince me of fleeting, seeing for his sake I break my fidelitie? Can he condemne me of disloyaltie, when he is the only cause of my disliking? May he iustly condemne me of trechery, who hath this testimony as tryal of my good wil? Doth not he remember that *the broken bone once set together, is stronger than euer it was?*

Kath. What is your crest? a coxcomb?
Pet. A combless cock, so Kate will be my hen.
Kath. No cock of mine; you crow too like a craven.
Taming the Shrew, Act ii. Scene 1.

Touch. Then learn this of me: to have, is to have; for it is a figure in rhetoric that drink, being poured out of a cup into a glass, by filling the one doth empty the other; for all your writers do consent that *ipse is he*: now, you are not ipse, for I am he.
As You Like It, Act v. Scene 1.

Though *Curio* bee as hot as a toast, yet *Euphues* is as colde as a clocke, though hee bee a cocke of the game, yet *Euphues* is content to bee *crauen* and crye creake, though *Curio* be olde huddle and twang, *ipse, he* yet *Euphues* had rather shrinke in the wetting than wast in the wearing. I know *Curio* to be steele to the backe, standerd bearer to *Venus* camp, sworne to the crew, true to ye crowne, knight marshall to *Cupid,* and heyre apparaunt to his kingdome.

Lucio. How now, noble Pompey! What, at the wheels of Cæsar? art thou led in triumph? What, is there none of *Pygmalion's images*, newly made *woman*, to be had now, for *putting the hand in the pocket and extracting it clutched?*
Measure for Measure, Act iii. Scene 2.

The *Lacedemonians* were wont to shewe their children dronken men and other wicked men, that by seing their filth, they might shunne the lyke fault, and auoyd the lyke vices when they were at the lyke state. The *Persians* to make their youth abhorre gluttony would paint an *Epicure* sleeping with meate in his mouth, and most horribly ouerladen with wine, that by the view of such monstrous sights, they might eschew the meanes of the lyke excesse. The *Parthians*, to cause their youth to loathe the alluring traines of womens wiles and deceiptful entisements, hadde most curiously carued in their houses, a young man blynde, besides whome was adioyned a *woman* so exquisite, that in some mens iudgement *Pygmalion's Image* was not halfe so excellent, hauing *one hande in his pocket as noting hir theft,* and holding a knife in the other hande to cut his throate.

Ros. I could find in my heart to disgrace my man's apparel and to cry like a woman; but I must comfort the *weaker vessel*, as doublet and hose ought to show itself courageous to petticoat: therefore courage, good Aliena!

As You Like it, Act ii. Scene 4.

Dull. Me, an 't shall please you; I am Anthony Dull.

King [*reads*]. 'For Jaquenetta,—so is *the weaker vessel* called which I apprehended with the aforesaid swain,—I keep her as a vessel of thy law's fury; and shall, at the least of thy sweet notice, bring her to trial.'

Love's Labour's Lost, Act i. Scene 1.

Host. By my troth, this is the old fashion; you two never meet but you fall to some discord: you are both, i' good truth, as rheumatic as two dry toasts; you cannot one bear with another's confirmities. What the good-year! one must bear, and that must be you: you are *the weaker vessel*, as they say, the emptier vessel.

2 Henry IV., Act ii. Scene 4.

Sam. A dog of that house shall move me to stand: I will take the wall of any man or maid of Montague's.

Gre. That shows thee a weak slave; for the weakest goes to the wall.

Sam. True; and therefore women, being the *weaker vessels*, are ever thrust to the wall; therefore I will push Montagu's men from the wall, and thrust his maids to the wall.

Romeo and Juliet, Act i. Scene 1.

Alas we silly soules which haue neither wit to decypher the wiles of men, nor wisdome to dissemble our affection, neither craft to traine in young louers, neyther courage to withstande their encounters, neither discretion to discerne their dubling, neither hard harts to reiect their complaints: we, I say, are soone enticed, beeing by nature simple, and easily entangled, beeing apte to receiue the impression of loue. But alas, it is both common and lamentable, to behold simplicity intrapped by subtilitie, and those that haue most might, to be infected with most mallice. The Spider weaueth a fine web to hang the Fly, the Wolfe weareth a faire face to deuour the Lambe, the Mirlin striketh at the Partridge, the Eagle often snappeth at the Fly, men are alwayes laying baites for women, which are the *weaker vessels*: but as yet I could neuer heare man by such snares to entrappe man: For true it is that men themselues haue by vse obserued, yat it must be a harde Winter when one wolfe cateth another.

Glou. We are the queen's *abjects*, and must obey.
Richard III., Act i. Scene 1.

Heere Ladies is a Glasse for all Princes to behold, that being called to dignitie, they vse moderation, not might, tempering the seueritie of the lawes, with the mildnes of loue, not executing all they wil, but shewing what they may. Happy are they, and onely they that are vnder this glorious and gracious Souereigntie: insomuch that I accompt all those *abiects* that be not hir subiectes.

Bru. There's no more to be said, but he is banish'd,
As enemy to the people and his country;
It shall be so.
 Citizens. It shall be so, it shall be so.
 Cor. You common cry of curs! whose breath I hate
As reek o' the rotten fens, whose loves I prize
As the dead carcasses of unburied men
That do corrupt my air, *I banish you.*
    Coriolanus, Act iii. Scene 3.

King Richard. You, cousin Hereford, upon pain of life,
Till twice five summers have enrich'd our fields
Shall not regret our fair dominions,
But tread the stranger paths of banishment.
 Boling. Your will be done: this must my comfort be,
That sun that warms you here shall shine on me;
And those his golden beams to you here lent
Shall point on me and gild my banishment.

. . . .

 Gaunt. Call it a travel that thou takest for pleasure.

Boling. My heart will sigh when I miscall it so,
Which finds it an inforced pilgrimage.
    Gaunt. The sullen passage of thy weary steps
Esteem as foil wherein thou art to set
The precious jewel of thy home return.
    Boling. Nay, rather, every tedious stride I make
Will but remember me what a deal of world
I wander from the jewels that I love.
Must I not serve a long apprenticehood
To foreign passages, and in the end,
Having my freedom, boast of nothing else
But that I was a journeyman to grief?
    *Gaunt. All places that the eye of heaven visits
Are to a wise man ports and happy havens.*
Teach thy necessity to reason thus;
There is no virtue like necessity.
*Think not the king did banish thee,
But thou the king.* Woe doth the heavier sit,
Where it perceives it is but faintly borne.
Go, say I sent thee forth to purchase honour
And not the king exiled thee; or suppose
Devouring pestilence hangs in our air
And thou art flying to a fresher clime:
Look, what thy soul holds dear, imagine it
To lie that way thou go'st, not whence thou
    comest:
Suppose the singing birds musicians,
The grass whereon thou treadest the presence strew'd,
The flowers fair ladies, and thy steps no more
Than a delightful measure or a dance;

For gnarling sorrow hath less power to bite
The man that mocks at it and sets it light.
Richard II., Act i. Scene 3.

If I were as wise to giue thee counsaile, as I am willing to do thee good, or as able to set thee at libertie as desirous to haue thee free, thou shouldest neither want good aduice to guide thee, nor sufficient help to restore thee. Thou takest it heauily that thou shouldest be accused without colour, and exiled without cause: and I thinke thee happy to be so well rid of the court and bee so voyde of crime. Thou sayst banishment is bitter to the free born, and I deeme it the better if thou bee without blame. There bee manye meates which are sower in the mouth and sharpe in the Mawe, but if thou mingle them with sweete sawces, they yeelde both a pleasaunt tast and wholesome nourishment. Diuers coulours offende the eyes, yet hauing greene among them, whette the sight. I speake this to this ende, that though thy exile seeme grieuous to thee, yet guiding thy selfe with the rules of Philosophie it shal bee more tollerable, hee that is colde doth not couer himselfe with care but with clothes, he that is washed in the rayne, dryeth himselfe by the fire, not by his fancie, and thou which art banished oughtest not with teares to bewayle thy hap, but with wisdome to heale thy hurt.

Nature hath giuen no man a country, no more then she hath a house or lands, or liuings. *Socrates* wold neither cal himself an *Athenian,* neither a *Græcian* but a citizen of ye world. *Plato* would neuer accompt him banished yat had he Sun, Fire, Aire, Water and Earth, that he had before, where he *felt the Winter's blast and the Summer's blaze*, where *ye same sun*, and the same moone *shined*, whereby he noted that *euery place was a country to a wise man*, and al parts a pallace to a quiet mind. But thou art driuen out of *Naples?* yat is nothing. All the *Athenians* dwel not in *Colliton*, nor euery *Corinthian* in *Græcia*, nor al the *Lacedemonians* in *Pitania*. How can any part of the world be distant farre from the other, when as the *Mathematicians* set down that the earth is but a point being compared to ye heauens. Learn of ye Bee as wel to gather Hunny of ye weede as the flowre, and out of farre countryes to liue, as wel as in thine own. He is to be laughed at which thincketh ye Moone better at *Athens* then at *Corinth*, or the Hunny of the Bee sweeter that is gathered in *Hybla*, then that which is made in *Mantua? when it was cast in Diogenes' teeth, yat the Sinoponetes had banished him Pontus. yea, said he, I them of Diogenes*. I may say to thee as *Straconicus* said to his guest, who demaunded what fault was punished with exile, and he aunswering false hoode, why then said *Straconicus* dost not thou practise deceit to the ende thou maist anoyd the misc[h]iefes that flow in thy country.

And surely if conscience be the cause thou art banished ye court, I accompt thee wise in being so precise yat by the vsing of vertue, thou maist be exciled the place of vice. Better it is for thee to liue with honesty in ye country then with honor in the court, and greater wil thy praise be in flying vanitie, then thy pleasure in followinge traines. Choose that place for thy pallace which is most quyet, custome will make it thy countrey, and an honest life will cause it a pleasaunt liuing. *Philip* falling in the dust, and seeing the figure of his shape perfect in shew. Good God, said he, we desire ye whole earth, and see howe little scrueth? *Zeno* hearing that this onely barke wherin all his wealth was shipped to haue perished, cryed out, thou hast done wel Fortune to thrust mee into my gowne againe to embrace Philosophye. Thou hast therefore in my minde great cause to reioyce, that God by punishment hath compelled thee to strictnesse of life, which by lybertie might haue ben growen to lewdnesse. When thou hast not one place assigned wherein to liue, but one forbidden thee which thou must leaue, then thou being denied but one, that excepted thou maist choose any. Moreouer this dispute with thy selfe, I beare no office wherby I should either for feare please the noble, or for gaine oppresse the needy. I am no arbiterer in doubtful cases, whereby I should either peruerte Iustice, or incurre displeasure. I am free from the iniuries of the stronge, and malice of the weak. I am out of the broyles of the seditious, and haue escaped the threates of the ambitious. But as hee that hauing a faire Orchard, seeing one tree blasted, recounteth the discommoditie of that, and passeth ouer in silence the fruitefulnesse of the other. So hee that is banyshed doth alwayes lament the losse of his house, and the shame of his *exile,* not reioysing at the liberty, quietnes and pleasure that he enioyeth by that *sweete punishment.* The kings of *Persia* were deemed happy in that they passed their Winter in *Babylon:* in *Media* their Summer, and their Spring in *Susis:* and certeinly the Exile in this may be as happy as any king in *Persia,* for he may at his leisure being at his owne pleasure, lead his Winter at *Athens,* his Summer in *Naples,* his Spring in *Argos.* But if he haue any busines in hand, he may study without trouble, sleepe without care, and wake at his wil without controlment. *Aristotle* must dine when it pleaseth *Philip. Diogenes* when it listeth *Diogenes,* the courtier suppeth when the king is satisfied, but *Botonio* may now eat when *Botonio* is an hungred. But thou saist that banishment is shamefull. No truely, no more then pouertie to the content, or grayc haires to the aged. It is the cause that maketh thee shame, if thou wert banished vpon choler, greater is thy credit in susteining wrong, then thy enuyes in committing iniury, and lesse shame is it to thee to be oppressed by might, then theirs that wrought it for malice. But thou fearest thou shalt not thriue in a straunge nation, certeinly thou art more afraide then hurte. The Pine tree groweth as soone in *Pharo* as in *Ida,* ye Nightingale singeth as sweetly in the descarts, as in ye woods of *Crete*. *The wise man liueth as wel in a far country as in his owne home.* It is not the nature of the place but the disposition of the person, that maketh the lyfe pleasant. Seeing therfore *Botonio*, that al the sea is apt for any fish, yat it is a bad ground where no flower wil grow, that *to a wise man all lands are as fertile as his owne enheritance*, I desire thee to temper the sharpnes of thy banishment with the sweetenes of the cause, and to measure the cleerenes of thyne owne conscience, with the spite of thy enimies' quarrel, so shalt thou reuenge their malyce with patience, and endure thy banishment with pleasure.

Euphues says, 'when it was cast in Diogenes' teeth that the Sinopontes had banished him Pontus, yea, said he, I them of Diogenes;' and Gaunt says, 'think not the king did banish thee, but thou the king;' and Coriolanus says to the citizens who had banished him, 'I banish you.' Euphues says, 'the *wise man* liveth as well in a far country as in his own home,' and that '*to a wise man all lands are as fertile as his own inheritance*,' and Shakespeare says, 'All places that the eye of heaven visits are *to a wise man* ports and happy havens.'

In 'As You Like It,' Act ii. Scene 1, the Duke Senior says:—

Now, my co-mates and brothers in *exile*,
Hath not old custom made this life more *sweet*
Than that of painted pomp? Are not these woods
More free from peril than the envious court?
Here *feel* we but the penalty of Adam,
The seasons' difference, as the icy fang
And churlish chiding of the winter's wind,
Which, when it bites and blows upon my body,
Even till I shrink with cold, I smile and say
' This is no flattery : these are counsellors
That feelingly persuade me what I am.'

And according to Lyly, Plato would never accompt him banished that had the sun, fire, air, water and earth, that he had before, where he *felt the winter's blast and summer's blaze*; in other words, where he felt the seasons' difference.

    K. John. Why, what a madcap hath heaven lent us here!
    Eli. He hath a trick of Cœur-de-lion's face ;
The accent of his tongue affecteth him.
Do you not read some tokens of my son
In the large *composition of this man?*
    K. John. Mine eye hath well examined his parts
And finds them perfect Richard.
              King John, Act i. Scene 1.

It hath bene a question often disputed, but neuer determined, whether the qualities of the minde, or the *composition of the man,* cause women most to lyke, or whether beautie or wit moue men most to loue. Certes by how much the more the minde is to be preferred before the body, by so much the more the graces of the one are to be preferred before ye gifts of ye other, which if it be so, that the contemplation of the *inward qualitie* ought to bee respected, more then the view of the *outward beautie,* then doubtlesse women either do or should loue those best whose vertue is best, not measuring the deformed man, with the reformed mind.

Sim. Opinion's but a fool, that makes us scan
The *outward habit* by the *inward man.*
Pericles, Act ii. Scene 2.

The foule Toade hath a faire stone in his head, the fine golde is found in the filthy earth: the sweet kernell lyeth in the hard shell : vertue is harboured in the heart of him that most men esteeme mishapen. Contrariwise, if we respect more the *outward shape,* then the *inward habit,* good God, into how many mischiefes do wee fall? into what blindnesse are we ledde ?

Sweet are the uses of adversity,
Which, like *the toad, ugly and venomous,*
Wears yet a precious jewel in his head.
As You Like It, Act. ii. Scene 1.

Thou sayest that all this is for loue, and that I

beeing thy friend, thou art loth to wink at my folly; truly I say with *Tully*, with faire wordes thou shalt yet perswade me: for experience teacheth me, that straight trees haue crooked rootes, smooth baites sharpe hookes, that *the fayrer the stone is in the Toade's head, the more pestilent the poyson is in hir bowelles*, that talk the more it is seasoned with fine phrases, the lesse it sauoreth of true meaning.

Boyet. Do not curst wives hold that self-sove-
reignty
Only for praise sake, when they strive to be
Lords o'er their lords?
 Prin. Only for praise: and praise we may af-
ford
To any lady that subdues a lord.
  Love's Labour's Lost, Act. iv. Scene 1.

They that feare to haue *curst wiues*, must not with rigour seeke to calme them, but saying gentle words in euery place by them, which maketh them more quyet.
Concerning the body, as there is no Gentlewoman so curious to haue him in print, so is there no one so careles to haue him a wretch, onlye his right shape to shew him a man, his Christendom to proue his faith, indifferent wealth to maintaine his family, ex-pecting all things necessary, nothing superfluous. And to conclude with you *Surius*, vnlesse I might haue such a one, I had as leaue be buried as maried,

wishing rather to haue no beautie and dye a chast virgin, then no ioy and liue a cursed wife.

D. Pedro. I will teach you how to humour your cousin, that she shall fall in love with Benedick; and I, with your two helps, will so practise on Benedick that, in despite of his quick wit and his *queasy stomach,* he shall fall in love with Beatrice.
    Much Ado About Nothing, Act ii. Scene 1.

I had thought *Philautus,* that a wounde healing so faire could neuer haue bred to a Fistula, or a bodye kept so well from drinke, to a dropsie, but I well perceiue that thy fleshe is as ranke as the wolues, who as soone as he is stricken recouereth a skinne, but rankleth inwardly vntill it come to the lyuer, and thy *stomacke as quesie* as olde *Nestors,* vnto whome pappe was no better then poyson, and thy body no lesse distempered then *Hermogineus,* whom abstinence from wine, made oftentimes dronken. I see thy humor is loue, thy quarrell iealousie, the one I gather by thine addle head, the other by thy suspicious nature: but I leaue them both to thy will and thee to thine owne wickednesse. Pretily to cloake thine own folly, thou callest me theese first, not vnlike vnto a curst wife, who deseruing a *check,** beginneth first to scolde.

Ang. What are you, sir?
Elb. He, sir! a tapster, sir; parcel-bawd; one that serves a bad woman; whose house, sir, was, as

---

* See p. 2, Aristotle's *Checks,* &c.

they say, plucked down in the suburbs; and now she professes a hot-house, which, I think, is a very ill house too.

Escal. How know you that?

Elb. My wife, sir, whom I detest before heaven and your honour,—

Escal. How? thy wife?

Elb. Ay, sir; whom, I thank heaven, is an honest woman,—

Escal. Dost thou detest her therefore?

Elb. I say, sir, I will detest myself also as well as she, that this house, if it be not a bawd's house, it is pity of her life, for it is a naughty house.

Escal. How dost thou know that, constable?

Elb. Marry, sir, by my wife; who, if she had been a woman *cardinally* given, might have been accused in fornication, adultery, and all uncleanliness there.

Measure for Measure, Act ii. Scene 1.

It is a world to see howe commonly we are blinded with the collusions of women, and more entised by their ornaments beeing artificiall, then their proportion beeinge naturall. I loath almost to thincke on their oyntments and appoticary drugges, the sleeking of their faces, and all their slibber sawces, whiche bring *quesinesse to the stomacke*, and disquiet to the minde.

Take from them their perywigges, their paintings, their Iewells, their rowles, their boulstrings, and thou shalt soone perceiue that a woman is the least parte of hir selfe. When they be once robbed of their robes, then wil they appeare so odious, so vgly, so monstrous, that thou wilt rather think them serpents than saints, and so like Hags, that thou wilt feare rather to be enchaunted then enamoured. Looke in their closettes, and there shalt thou finde an Appoticaryes shop of sweete confections, a surgions boxe of sundry salues, a Pedlers packe of newe fangles. Besides all this their shadowes, their spots, their lawnes, their leefe-kyes, their ruffes, their rings: Shew them rather *Cardinalls* curtisans, then modest Matrons, and more *carnally* affected, then moued in conscience. If euery one of these things scuverally be not of force to moue thee, yet all of them ioyntly should mortifie thee.

' King Henry VIII. suppressed all the stews or brothel-houses, which long had continued on the Bankside in Southwark. And those infamous women were not buried in Christian burial when they were dead, nor permitted to receive the rites of the Church whilst they lived.

' Before the reign of Henry VIII. there were eighteen of these infamous houses, and Henry VIII. for a time forbad them; but afterwards twelve only were permitted, and had *signs painted on their walls*, as a *Boar's head*, the Cross keys, the Gun, the *Castle*, the Crane, the *Cardinal's hat*, the Bell, the Swan, &c.'—*Coke* 3, *Institute*, cap. xcviii.

Coke gives the names of eight of the twelve brothels which were permitted; and to one of them, the Castle, Shakespeare may allude in this passage:—

Fal. By the Lord, thou sayest true, lad. And is not my hostess of the tavern a most sweet wench?
Prince. As the honey of Hybla, my old lad of the castle.
1 *Henry IV.*, Act i. Scene 1.

Prince Henry calls Falstaff 'my old lad of the castle,' implying probably that he frequented a house which had the name of one of the twelve, and therefore likely to be well known, by reputation at least, to the frequenters of the Globe Theatre. In the same scene, the Prince also refers to the signs mentioned by Coke :—

Prince. What a devil hast thou to do with the time of the day? Unless hours were cups of sack and minutes capons and clocks the tongues of bawds and dials *the signs of leaping-houses* and the blessed sun himself a fair hot wench in flame-coloured

taffeta, I see no reason why thou shouldst be so superfluous to demand the time of the day.
1 *Henry IV.*, Act i. Scene 1.

Shakespeare and Lyly both play upon the word cardinal, and they probably allude to the Cardinal's hat mentioned by Coke, so that a frequenter of the Cardinal's hat might be said to be both cardinally and carnally given. Moreover, Lyly speaks of Cardinal's curtisans:

Win. How now, ambitious Humphry! what means this?
Glou. Peel'd priest, dost thou command me to be shut out?
Win. I do, thou most usurping proditor,
And not protector of the king or realm.
Glou. Stand back, thou manifest conspirator,
Thou that contrivedst to murder our dead lord;
Thou that givest *whores* indulgences to sin;
I'll canvass thee in thy broad *cardinal's hat*,
If thou proceed in this thy insolence.

And Gloucester says to the Bishop of Winchester, afterwards Cardinal:—

Thou that givest whores indulgences to sin:
I'll canvass thee in thy broad *cardinal's hat.*

Prince. Where sups he? doth the old boar feed in the old frank?

Bard. At the old place, my lord, in Eastcheap.

2 *Henry IV.*, Act ii. Scene 2.

Shakespeare here refers to the Boar's head, which was a tavern in Eastcheap, a scene in this play, and the name of one of the infamous houses mentioned by Coke.

His curses, then from *bitterness of soul*
Denounced against thee, are all fall'n upon thee;
And God, not we, hath plagued thy bloody deed.

Richard III., Act. i. Scene 3.

I will not vse many wordes, for if thou be wise, few are sufficient, if froward, superfluous; one lyne is inough, if thou be courteous, one word too much, if thou be cruell. Yet this I adde and that in *bitterness of soule*, that neither my hande dareth write that, which my heart intendeth, nor my tongue vtter that, which my hande shall execute. And so fare-well, vnto whom onely I wish well.

Mess. I see, lady, the gentleman is *not in your books.*

Beat. No; an he were, I would burn my study.

Much Ado About Nothing, Act i. Scene 1.

If I were as farre *in thy bookes* to be beleeued, as

thou art in mine to be beloued, thou shouldest either soone be made a wife, or euer remaine a Virgin, the one would ridde me of hope, the other acquit mee of feare.

———

Gru. Why, therefore fire ; for I have caught extreme cold. Where's the cook? is supper ready, the house trimmed, *rushes strewed,* cobwebs swept ; the serving-men in their new fustian, their white stockings, and every officer his wedding-garment on?
Taming the Shrew, Act iv. Scene 1.

Sir To. O knight, thou lackest a cup of canary : when did I see thee so put down?
Sir And. Never in your life, I think: unless you see canary put me down. Methinks sometimes I have no more wit than a Christian or an ordinary man has : but I am *a great eater of beef* and I believe that *does harm to my wit.*
Sir To. No question.
Twelfth Night, Act i. Scene 3.

Ther. With too much blood and too little brain, these two may run mad : but, if with too much brain and too little blood they do, I'll be a curer of madmen. Here's Agamemnon, an honest fellow enough, and one that loves *quails*; but he has not so much brain as ear-wax : and the goodly transformation of Jupiter there, his brother, the bull, —the primitive statue, and oblique memorial of cuckolds; a thrifty shoeing-horn in a chain, hanging at his brother's leg,—to what form but that he is, should wit larded with malice and malice forced with wit turn him to?

  Troilus and Cressida, Act v. Scene 1.

I am sory *Euphues* that we haue no *greene Rushes*, considering you haue beene so great a straunger, you make me almost to thinke that of you which commonly I am not accustomed to iudge of any, that either you thought your selfe too good, or our cheere too badde, other cause of absence I cannot imagine, vnlesse seeing vs very idle, you sought meanes to be well imployed, but I pray you hereafter be bolde, and those thinges which were amisse shall be redressed, for we will haue *Quailes* to amende your commons, and some *questions* to sharpen your wittes, so that you shall neither finde faulte with your *dyot* for the grosenesse, nor with your exercise for the easinesse. As for your fellowe and friende *Philautus* we are bounde to him, for he would oftentimes see vs, but seldome eate with vs, which made vs thinke that he cared more for our company, then our meat.

 Euphues as one that knewe his good, aunswered hir in this wise.

 Fayre Ladye, it were vnseemely to *strewe greene rushes* for his comming, whose companie is not worth a strawe, or to accompt him a straunger whose boldnesse hath bin straunge to all those that knew him to be a straunger.

 The small abilitie in me to requite, compared with the great cheere I receiued, might happlie make me refraine, which is contrary to your coniecture: Neither was I euer so busied in any weightie affaires, whiche I accompted not as lost time in respect of the exercise I alwayes founde in your company, whiche maketh me thinke that your latter obiection proceeded rather to conuince mee for a treuant, then to manyfest a trueth.

As for the Quailes you promise me, I can be content with *beefe*, and for the questions they must be easie, els shall I not aunswere them, for my *wit* will shew with what grosse *diot* I haue beene brought vp, so that conferring my rude replyes with my base birth, you will thinke that meane cheare will serue me, and resonable questions deceiue me, so that I shall neither finde fault for my repast, nor fauour for my reasons.

. . . .

For as the Bee that gathereth Honnye out of the weede, when shee espieth the fayre floure flyeth to the sweetest: or as the kinde spaniell though he hunt after Birds, yet forsakes them to retriue the Partridge: or as we commonly feede on *beefe* hungerly at the first, yet seeing the *Quaile* more daintie, chaunge our dyet.

. . . .

My good sonne though thou wilt not suffer mee to perswade thee, yet shalt thou not let mee to pittie thee, yea and to pray for thee: but the tyme will come when comming home by weeping crosse, thou shalt confesse, that it is better to be at home in the caue of an Hermit then abroad in the court of an

Emperour, and that a crust with quietnesse, shall be better then *Quayles* with vnrest. And to the ende thou maist prone my sayings as true, as I know thyselfe to bee wilfull, take the paines to retourne by to this poore Cell, where thy fare shall be amended, if thou amende thy fault, and so farewell.

Sir Andrew says, 'I am a great eater of *beef*, and I believe that does harm to my *wit*.' And Euphues says, 'I can be content with beef, and for the questions they must be easy, else shall I not answer them, for my wit will shew with what gross diet I have been brought up.' 'Although Agamemnon loves quails, yet he has not so much brain as earwax.'

Ther. The plague of Greece upon thee, thou mongrel *beef-witted* lord!
Troilus and Cressida, Act ii. Scene 1.

Thersites calls 'blockish Ajax' beef-witted Lord.

Ulysses. No, make a lottery;
And, by device, let *blockish* Ajax draw
The sort to fight with Hector.
Troilus and Cressida, Act i. Scene 3.

Were it not, my sonnes, that Nature worketh

more in me then Iustice, I should disherite the one of you, who promiseth by his folly to spende all, and leaue the other nothing, whose wisedome seemeth to purchase all things. But I well know, that a bitter roote is amended with a sweete graft, and crooked trees proue good Cammocks, and wilde Grapes make pleasaunt Wine. Which perswadeth me, that thou (poynting to me) wilt in age repent thy youthful affections, and learne to dye as well, as thou hast liued wantonly. As for thee (laying his hande on my brother's head) although I see more than commonly in any of thy yeares, yet knowing that those that giue themselues to be bookish, are oftentimes so *blockish*, that they forget thrift: Where-by the olde Saw is verified, that the greatest Clearkes are not the wisest men, who digge still at the roote, while others gather the fruite, I am determined to helpe thee forward, least hauing nothing thou desire nothing, and so be accompted as no body.

Claud. For the which she wept heartily and said she cared not.

D. Pedro. Yea, that she did; but yet, for all that, an *if she did not hate him deadly, she would love him dearly:* the old man's daughter told us all.

Much Ado About Nothing, Act v. Scene 1.

Lucilla not ashamed to confesse hir folly, aunswered him with this frumpe.

Sir, whether your deserts or my desire haue

wrought this chaunge, it will boote you lyttle to know, neither do I craue amends, neither feare reuenge: as for feruent loue, you know there is no fire so hotte but it is quenched with water, neither affection so strong but is weakened with reason, let this suffice thee, that thou knowe I care not for thee.

In deede (said *Euphues*) to know the cause of your alteracion would boote me lyttle, seing the effect taketh such force. I haue heard that *women either loue entirely or hate deadly*, and seeing you haue put me out of doubt of the one, I must needes perswade myselfe of the other. This chaunge will cause *Philautus* to laugh me to scorne, and double thy lightnesse in tourning so often. Such was the hope that I conceiued of thy constancie, that I spared not in all places to blaze thy loyaltie, but now my rash conceipt wil proue me a lyer, and thee a lyght huswife.

Arch.   Let us on,
And publish the occasion of our arms.
The commonwealth is sick of their own choice;
Their over-greedy love hath surfeited;
An habitation giddy and unsure
Hath he that buildeth on the vulgar heart.
O thou fond many, with what loud applause
Didst thou beat heaven with blessing Bolingbroke,
Before he was what thou wouldst have him be!
And being now trimm'd in thine own desires,

Thou, beastly feeder, art so full of him,
That thou provokest thyself to cast him up.
So, so, *thou common dog, didst thou disgorge
Thy glutton bosom of the royal Richard;
And now thou wouldst eat thy dead vomit up,*
And howl'st to find it.
                    2 *Henry IV.*, Act i. Scene 3.

With what face *Euphues* canst thou *returne to thy vomit, seeming with the greedy hounde to lap vp that which thou diddest cast vp.*

Pol. Yet here, Laertes! aboard, aboard, for shame!
The wind sits in the shoulder of your sail,
And you are stay'd for.   There; my blessing with thee!
And *these few precepts* in thy memory.
See thou character.   Give thy thoughts no tongue,
Nor any unproportioned thought his act.
Be thou familiar, but by no means vulgar.
Those friends thou hast, and their adoption tried,
Grapple them to thy soul with hoops of steel;
But do not dull thy palm with entertainment
Of each new-hatch'd, unfledged comrade.   Beware
Of entrance to a quarrel, but being in,
Bear't that the opposed may beware of thee.
Give every man thy ear, but few thy voice:
Take each man's censure, but reserve thy judgment.

Costly thy habit as thy purse can buy,
But not express'd in fancy; rich, not gaudy.
Hamlet, Act i. Scene 3.

And to thee *Philautus* I begin to addresse my speach, hauing made an end of mine hermits tale, and if *these few precepts* I giue thee be obserued, then doubt not but we both shall learne that we best lyke. And these they are.

At thy comming into *England* be not too inquisitiue of newes, neither curious in matters of State, in assemblies aske no questions, either concerning manners or men. Be not lauish of thy tongue, either in causes of weight, least thou shew thy selfe an espyall, or in wanton talke, least thou proue thy selfe a foole.

It is the Nature of that country to sift straungers: euery one that shaketh thee by the hand, is not ioyned to thee in heart. They thinke *Italians* wanton, and *Grecians* subtill, they will trust neither they are so incredulous: but vndermine both, they are so wise. Be not quarrellous for euery lyght occasion: they are impatient in their anger of any equal, readie to reuenge an iniury, but neuer wont to profer any: they neuer fight without prouoking, and once prouoked they neuer cease. Beware thou fal not into ye snares of loue, ye women there are wise, the men craftie: they will gather loue by thy lookes, and picke thy minde out of thy hands. It shal be there better to heare what they say, then to speak what thou thinkest.

This advice of Euphues to Philautus is probably the origin of the advice of Polonius to Laertes.

I will place some parts of these passages close together, so that the reader will more easily see the resemblance between *these few precepts* of Euphues and Polonius.

Polonius.—Give thy thoughts no tongue.

Euphues.—Be not lavish of thy tongue.

Polonius.—Do not dull thy palm with entertainment of each new-hatch'd unfledged comrade.

Euphues.—Every one that shaketh thee by the hand, is not joined to thee in heart.

Polonius.—Beware of entrance to a quarrel, but being in, bear't that the opposed may beware of thee.

Euphues.—Be not quarrellous for every light occasion: they never fight without provoking, and once provoked they never cease. *Beware,* &c.

Polonius.—Give every man thine ear, but few thy voice.

Euphues.—It shall be there better to hear what they say, then to speak what thou thinkest.

The word *beware* is used by Lyly and Shakespeare in these passages.

There is further resemblance to the advice of Polonius in other parts of Euphues, but I cannot now quote all of them.

Descende into your owne consciences, consider with your selues the great difference between staring and starke blynde, witte and wisedome, loue and lust. Be merry but with modestie, be sober but not too sullen: be valiaunt, but not too venterous: let your attire be comely, but not too *costly*: your dyet wholesome, but not excessiue: vse pastime as the word importeth, to passe ye time in honest recreation: mistrust no man without cause, neither be ye credulous without proofe: be not lyght to follow euery mans opinion, neither obstinate to stand in your owne conceipts.

Polonius.—*Costly* thy habit as thy purse can buy, but not expressed in fancy.

Euphues.—Let your attire be comely, but not *costly*.

Lear. What hast thou been?
Edg. A serving-man, proud in heart and mind; that *curled my hair.*
Lear, Act. iii. Scene 4.

Ner. What say you then, to Falconbridge, the young baron of England?

Por. You know I say nothing to him, for he understands not me, nor I him: he hath neither Latin, French, nor Italian, and you will come into the court and swear that I have a poor pennyworth in the English. He is a proper man's picture, but, alas, who can converse with a dumb-show? How oddly he is suited! *I think he bought his doublet in Italy, his round hose in France, his bonnet in Germany,* and his behaviour every where.

Merchant of Venice, Act i. Scene 2.

Shakespeare may in this passage allude to the 'inconstancy of attire' in England, thus described in Euphues.

The attire they vse is rather ledde by the imitation of others, then their owne inuention, so that there is nothing in Englande more constant, then the inconstancie of attire, nowe vsing the French fashion, nowe the Spanish, then the Morisco gownes, then one thing, then another, insomuch that in drawing of an English man ye paynter setteth him downe naked, hauing in ye one hande a payre of sheares, in the other a piece of cloath, who hauing cut his choler after the French guise is readie to make his sleeue after the Barbarian manner. And although this were the greatest enormitie that I coulde see in Englande, yet is it to be excused, for they that cannot maintaine this pride must leaue of necessitie, and they that be able, will leaue when they see the vanitie.

Beware of solitarinesse. But although I would haue thee vse company for thy recreation, yet woulde I haue thee alwayes to leaue the companye of those that accompany thy Lady, yea, if she haue any iewell of thine in hir custodie, rather loose it then goe for it, least in seeking to recouer a trifle, thou renewe thine olde trouble. *Be not curious to curle thy haire,* nor carefull to be neat in thine apparel, be not prodigal of thy golde, nor precise in thy going, be not *lyke the Englishman, which preferreth euery straunge fashion before the vse of his countrey,* be thou dissolute, least thy Lady thinke thee foolish in framing thy selfe to euerye fashion for hir sake. Beleeue not their othes and solempne protestations, their exorcismes and coniurations, their teares which they haue at commaundement, their alluring lookes, their treading on the toe, their vnsauery toyes.

Kath. What, will you not suffer me? Nay, now
    I see
She is your treasure, she must have a husband;
I must dance bare-foot on her wedding day
And for your love to her *lead apes in hell.*
       Taming the Shrew, Act ii. Scene 1.

Leon. You may light on a husband that hath no beard.

Beat. What should I do with him? dress him in my apparel and make him my waiting-gentlewoman. He that hath a beard is more than a youth, and he

E

that hath no beard is less than a man : and he that is more than a youth is not for me, and he that is less than a man, I am not for him : therefore I will even take sixpence in earnest of the bear-ward, and *lead his apes into hell.*

Leon. Well, then, go you into hell ?

Beat. No, but to the gate ; and there will the devil meet me, like an old cuckold, with horns on his head ; and say, ' Get you to heaven, Beatrice, get you to heaven ; here's no place for you maids ;' so deliver I up my apes, and away to Saint Peter for the heavens; he shows me where the bachelors sit, and there live we as merry as the day is long.

Much Ado About Nothing, Act ii. Scene 1.

Therefore *Lucilla,* if thou haue any care to be a comfort to my hoary haires, or a commoditie to thy common weale, frame thy self to that honourable estate of Matrimony, which was sanctified in Paradise, allowed of the Patriarches, hallowed of the olde Prophets, and commended of al persons. If thou lyke any, be not ashamed to tell it me, which onely am to exhort thee, yea and as much as in me lyeth to commaunde thee, to loue one: If he be base, thy bloud will make him noble: If beggerly, thy goods shall make him wealthy : If a straunger thy freedome may enfraunchise him : If he be young, he is the more fitter to be thy pheere : if he be olde, the lyker to thine aged father. For I had rather thou shouldest leade a lyfe to thine owne lyking in earthe, then to thy great torments, *lead Apes in*

Hell. Be bolde therefore to make me partaker of thy desyre, which will be partaker of thy disease: yea, and a furtherer of thy delightes, as farre as either my friendes, or my landes, or my life will stretch.

I neuer heard but of three things which argued a fine wit, Inuention, Conceiuing, Aunswering. Which haue all bene found so common in women, that were it not I should flatter them, I should think them singular.

Then this sufficeth me, that my seconde daughter shall not *lead Apes in Hell*, though she haue not a penny for the Priest, bicause she is wittie, which bindeth weake things, and looseth strong things, and worketh all things, in those that haue either wit themselues, or loue wit in others.

When the Foxe preacheth, the Geese perish. The Crocodile shrowdeth greater treason vnder most pitiful teares: in a kissing mouth there lyeth a galling minde. You haue made so large profer of your seruice, and so faire promises of fidelytie, that were I not ouer charie of mine honestie, you woulde inueigle me to shake handes with chastitie. But certes I will either lead a virgin's life in earth (though *I lead Apes in hel*), or els follow thee rather then thy gifts: yet am I neither so precise to refuse thy profer, neither so peeuish to disdain thy good wil: so excellent alwayes are the gifts which are made acceptable by the vertue of ye giuer.

Beat. Who is his companion now? He hath every month a new sworn brother.

Mess. Is't possible?

Beat. Very easily possible; *he wears his faith but as the fashion of his hat; it ever changes with the next block.*

Much Ado About Nothing, Act i. Scene 1.

But thy friendship *Philautus* is lyke a new fashion, which being vsed in the morning, is accompted olde before noone, which varietie of chaunging, being oftentimes noted of a graue gentleman in *Naples*, who hauing bought a *Hat of the newest fashion*, and best *block* in all *Italy*, and wearing but one daye, it was tolde him yat it was stale, he hung it vp in his studie, and viewing al sorts, al shapes, perceiued at ye last, his olde Hat againe to come into the new fashion, where-with, smiling to himselfe he sayde, I haue now lyued compasse, for *Adam's* olde Apron, must make *Eue* a new kirtle: noting this, that when no new thing could be deuised, nothing could be more new then ye olde. I speake this to this ende *Philautus*, yat I see thee as often chaunge thy head as others do their Hats, now beeing friend to *Aiax*, bicause he shoulde couer thee with his buckler, now to *Vlysses*, that he may pleade for thee with his eloquence, now to one and nowe to an other, and thou dealest with thy friendes, as that Gentleman did with his felt, for seeing not my vaine, aunswerable to thy vanities, thou goest about (but yet the neerest way) to hang me vp for holydayes, as one neither fitting thy head nor pleasing thy humor, but when *Philautus* thou shalt see that chaunge of friendships shal make thee a fat calfe, and a leane Cofer, that there is no more hold in a new friend then a new fashion, yat *Hats alter as fast as the Turner can turne his block,* and harts as soone as one can turne his back, when seeing euery one return to his olde wearing, and finde it ye best, then compelled rather for want of others, then good wil of me, thou wilt retire to *Euphues,* whom thou laydest by ye wals, and seeke him againe as a new friend, saying to thy self, I haue lyued compasse, *Euphues'* olde *faith* must make *Philautus* a new friend.

Beatrice says, 'he wears his *faith* but as the fashion of his hat; it ever changes with the next block,' and Lyly says, 'hats alter as fast as the turner can turn his block,' and that 'Euphues' old *faith* must make Philautus a new friend.'

 Lear. When we are born, we cry that we are
  come
To this great stage of *fools.* This a good *block*?
It were a delicate stratagem, to shoe
A troop of horse with *felt.*
     Lear, Act iv. Scene 6.

Lear connects the word 'fool' with the word

'block' as it is used in the 'Two Gentlemen of Verona,' Act ii. Scene 5,—

Speed. What an ass art thou! I understand thee not.

Launce. What a *block* art thou, that thou canst not! My staff understands me.

Signifying a foolish person or blockhead, and the word 'felt' with the hatter's block.

It is also requisite that he be expert in marcyall affayres, in shootinge, in dartinge, that he hauke and hunte for his honest pastime and recreation, and if after these pastimes hee shall seeme secure, nothing regardinge his bookes, I woulde not haue him scourged with stripes, but threatened with wordes, not dulled with blowes, lyke seruaunts, the which the more they are beaten the better they beare it, and the lesse they care for it, for children of good disposition are either incited by praise to goe forward, or shamed by dispraise to commit the like offence: those of obstinate and *blockish* behauiour, are neither with wordes to be perswaded, neither with stripes to bee corrected.

Helena. O, is it all forgot?
All school-days' friendship, childhood innocence?
We, Hermia, like two artificial gods,
Have with our needles created both one flower,
Both on *one* sampler, sitting on *one* cushion,

THE FRIENDSHIP OF HELENA AND HERMIA. 55

Both warbling of *one* song, both in *one* key,
As if our hands, our sides, voices and minds,
Had been incorporate. *So we grew together*,
Like to a double cherry, seeming parted,
But yet an union in partition;
Two lovely berries moulded on one stem;
So, with two seeming bodies, but one heart;
Two of the first, like coats in heraldry,
Due but to one and crowned with one crest.
Midsummer Night's Dream, Act iii. Scene 2.

Either *Euphues* and *Philautus* stoode in neede of friendshippe, or were ordeined to be friendes: vpon so short warning, to make so soone fine, a conclusion might seeme in mine opinion of it continued myraculous, if shaken off, ridiculous.

But after many embracings and protestations one to another, they walked to dinner, wher they wanted neither meat, neither Musicke, neither any other pastime: and hauing banqueted, to digest their sweete confections, they daunced all that after noone, they vsed not onely *one* boorde but *one* bed, *one* booke (if so be it they thought not one too many.) *Their friendship augmented euery day*, insomuch that the one could not refraine the company of the other one minute, all things went in common betweene them, which all men accompted commendable.

Lyly's account of the friendship of Euphues and Philautus may have suggested Shakespeare's beautiful description of the school-days' friendship of Helena and Hermia.

Jul. Thou know'st the mask of night is on my face,
Else would a maiden blush bepaint my cheek
For that which thou hast heard me speak to-night.
Fain would I dwell on form, fain, fain deny
What I have spoke: but farewell compliment!
Dost thou love me? I know thou wilt say 'Ay,'
And I will take thy word: yet, if thou swear'st,
Thou mayst prove false; at lovers' perjuries,
They say, Jove laughs. O gentle Romeo,
If thou dost love, pronounce it faithfully:
Or *if thou think'st I am too quickly won,*
I'll frown and be perverse, and say thee nay,
So thou wilt woo; but else, not for the world.
In truth, fair Montague, I am too fond,
And therefore thou mayst think my 'haviour *light*:
But trust me, *gentleman,* I'll prove more true
Than those that have more cunning to be strange.
Romeo and Juliet, Act ii. Scene 2.

Thus not blinded by light affection, but dazeled with your rare perfection, and boldened by your exceeding courtesie: I haue vnfolded mine entire loue, desiring you hauing so good leasure, to giue so friendlye an aunswere, as I may recciue comforte, and you commendacion.

Lucilla, although she were contented to heare this

desired discourse, yet did shee seeme to bee somewhat displeased. And truely I know not whether it be peculiar to that sexe to dissemble with those whom they most desire, or whether by craft they haue learned outwardly to loath that, which inwardly they most loue: yet wisely did she cast this in hir head, that *if she should yeelde at the first assault, he would thinke hir a light huswife.* : if she should reiect him scornfully a very haggard: minding therefore that he shoulde neither take holde of hir promise, neither vnkindenesse of hir preciseneese, she fed him indifferently, with hope and dispaire, reason and affection, life and death. Yet in the ende arguing wittily vpon certeine questions, they fel to such agreement, as poore *Philautus* would not haue agreed vnto if he had ben present, yet alwayes keeping the body vndefiled. And thus she replied:

Gentleman, as you may suspect me of idlenesse in giuing eare to your talke, so may you conuince me of *lightnesse* in annswering such toyes: certes as you haue made *mine eares glow at the rehearsall of your loue,* so haue you galled my heart with ye remembraunce of your folly. Though you came to *Naples* as a straunger, yet were you welcome to my fathers house as a friend: And can you then so much transgresse the bonds of honour (I will not say of honestie,) as to solicite a sute more sharpe to me then death? I haue hetherto God bee thanked, lyued without suspition of lewdenesse, and shall I now incurre the daunger of sensual libertie?

. . . .

Lucilla seemed to be somewhat displeased with the love-making of Philautus, and thought that if she yielded at the first assault, he would think her a *light* huswife; and Juliet says:—

If thou think'st I am too quickly won,
I'll frown and be perverse and say thee nay,
. . . .
Thou mayst think my 'haviour *light*.

Lucilla's ears glow at the rehearsal of the love of Philautus; a maiden blush bepaints Juliet's cheek for what Romeo had heard her speak that night; and Lucilla and Juliet address their lovers as 'gentleman.'

    Jul. Three words, dear Romeo, and good night indeed.
If that *thy bent* of love be honourable,
Thy purpose marriage, send me word to-morrow,
By one that I'll procure to come to thee,
Where and what time thou wilt perform the rite;
And all my fortunes at thy foot I'll lay
And follow thee my lord throughout the world.
    Romeo and Juliet, Act ii. Scene 2.

What hope can you haue to obteine my loue, seeing yet I could neuer affoord you a good looke? Do you therefore thinke me easely entised to the *bent of your bow*, bicause I was easely entreated to listen to your late discourse?

Lucilla asks Philautus, whether he thinks her easily enticed to the *bent* of his bow, and Juliet asks Romeo if his '*bent* of love be honourable.'

 Fri. L. God pardon sin! wast thou with Rosaline?
 Rom. With Rosaline, my ghostly father? no; I have forgot that name, and that name's woe.
    Romeo and Juliet, Act ii. Scene 3.

Tush *Philautus* was liked for fashion sake, but neuer loued for fancie sake: and this I vowe by the faith of a Virgin, and by the loue I beare thee, (for greater bands to confirme my vow I haue not) that my father shall sooner martir mee in the fire then marye mee to *Philautus*. No no, *Euphues*, thou onely hast wonne me by loue, and shalt onely weare me by law: I force not *Philautus* his fury, so I may haue *Euphues* his friendship: neither wil I prefer his possessions before thy person, neither esteme better of his lands, then of thy loue. *Ferardo* shall sooner disherite me of my patrimony, then dishonour me in breaking my promise? It is not his great *mannors*, but thy good *manners*, that shall make my marriage. In token of which my sincere affection, I giue thee my hande in pawne, and my heart for euer to be thy *Lucilla*.

Romeo loved Rosaline before he saw Juliet, and Lucilla loved Philautus before she saw Euphues; and yet it has been said, that 'this drama affords a strong instance of the fineness of Shakespeare's insight into the nature of the passions, that Romeo is introduced already love-bewildered.' *

Biron. In what manner?
Cost. In manner and form following, sir; all those three: I was seen with her in the *manor-house*, sitting with her upon the form, and taken following her into the park; which, put together, is in *manner* and form following. Now, sir, for the *manner*,—it is the *manner* of a man to speak to a woman: for the form,—in some form.
Love's Labour's Lost, Act i. Scene 1.

The Rose that is eaten with the Canker is not gathered bicause it groweth on that stalke yat the sweet doth, neither was *Helen* made a Starre, bicause shee came of that Egge with *Castor,* nor thou a gentleman in yat thy auncestours were of nobilitie. It is not ye descent of birth but ye consent of conditions that maketh Gentlemen, neither great *manors* but good *manners* that expresse the true Image of dignitie.

. . . .

A gentleman that hath honest and discreet seruants

* Coleridge.

dysposeth them to the encrease of his Segnioryes, one he appointeth stewarde of his courtes, an other ouerseer of his landes, one his factor in far countries for his merchaundize, an other puruayour for his cates at home. But if among all his seruants he shal espy one, either filthy in his talke or foolish in his behauior, either without wit or voyde of honestye, either an vnthrift or a wittall, him he sets not as a suruayour and ouerseer of his *manors,* but a superuisour of hys childrens conditions and *manners,* to him he committeth ye guiding and tuition of his sons, which is by his proper nature a slaue, a knaue by condition, a beast in behauior. And sooner will they bestow an hundreth crownes to haue a horse well broken, then a childe well taught, wherein I cannot but maruell to see them so careful to encrease their possessions, when they be so carelesse to haue them wise that should inherite them.

Rom. And stay, good nurse, behind the abbey wall:
Within this hour my man shall be with thee,
And bring thee cords made like a tackled stair;
Which to the high top-gallant of my joy
Must be my convoy in the secret night.
Farewell; be trusty, and I'll quit thy pains:
Farewell; commend me to thy mistress.
　Nurse. Now God in heaven bless thee! Hark you, sir.
　Rom. What say'st thou, my dear nurse?

Nurse. Is your man secret? Did you ne'er
hear say,
Two may keep counsel putting one away?
Rom. I warrant thee, my man's as true as steel.
Romeo and Juliet, Act ii. Scene 4.

And verily if I had not loued thee well, I would
haue swallowed mine own sorrow in silence, knowing
yat in loue nothing is so daungerous as to perticipate
the meanes thereoff to an other, and that *two may
keepe counsaile if one be away,* I am therefore enforced perforce, to challenge that curtesie at thy
hands, which earst thou didst promise with thy
heart, the performaunce whereoff shall binde me to
Philautus, and prooue thee faithful to *Euphues.*

Nurse. Pray you, sir, a word: and as I told you,
my young lady bade me inquire you out; what she
bade me say, I will keep to myself: but first let me
tell ye, if ye should *lead her into a fool's paradise,*
as they say, it were a very gross kind of behaviour,
as they say: for the gentlewoman is young; and,
therefore, if you should deal double with her, truly
it were an ill thing to be offered to any gentlewoman, and very weak dealing.
Romeo and Juliet, Act ii. Scene 4.

The eye that blindeth thee, shall make thee see,
the Scorpion that stung thee shall heale thee, a
sharpe sore hath a short cure, let vs goe: to the
which *Euphues* consented willyngly, smiling to him-

selfe to see how he had brought *Philautus,* into a *fooles Paradise.*

Gentleman, if the inward spirite be aunswerable to the outward speach, or the thoughtes of your heart agreeable to the words of your mouth, you shall breede to your selfe great discredite, and to me no small disquyet. Do you thinke Gentleman that the minde being created of God, can be ruled by man, or that anye one can moue the heart, but he that made the heart? But such hath bene the superstition of olde women, and such the folly of young men, yat there could be nothing so vayne but the one woulde inuent, nor anye thing so seneelesse but the other would beleeue: which then brought youth *into a fooles Paradise,* and hath now cast age into an open mockage.

Tra. Shall sweet Bianca practise how to *bride it?*
Taming of the Shrew, Act. iii. Scene 2.

Cap. God's bread! it makes me mad:
Day, night, hour, tide, time, work, play,
Alone, in company, still *my care hath been*
To have her match'd : and having now provided
A gentleman of noble parentage,
Of fair demesnes, youthful, and nobly train'd,
Stuff'd, as they say, with honourable parts,
Proportion'd as one's thought would wish a man.
    Romeo and Juliet, Act ii. Scene 5.

But as *Ferardo* went in post, so hee retourned in

hast hauing concluded with *Philautus,* that the *marriage should immediately be consummated,* which wrought such a content in *Philautus,* that he was almost in an extasie through the extremitie of his passions: such is the fulnesse and force of pleasure, that ther is nothing so daungerous as the fruition, yet knowing that delayes bring daungers, although hee nothing doubted of *Lucilla* whome hee loued, yet feared he the ficklenesse of olde men, which is alwayes to be mistrusted.

Hee vrged therefore *Ferardo* to breake with his Daughter, who beeing willyng to haue the matche made, was content incontinentlye to procure the meanes: finding therefore his daughter at leisure, and hauing knowledge of hir former loue, spake to hir as followeth.

Deere daughter as thou hast long time liued a maiden, so now thou must learne to be a Mother, and as I haue bene carefull to bring thee vp a Virgin, so am I now desirous to make thee a Wife. Neither ought I in this matter to vse any perswasions, for that maidens commonly now a dayes are no sooner borne, but they beginne to *bride it*: neither to offer any great portions, for that thou knowest thou shalt enherite al my possessions. *Mine onely care hath bene hetherto, to match thee* with such an one, as shoulde be of good wealth, able to mainteine thee: of great worship, able to compare with thee in birth: of honest conditions, to deserue thy loue: and an *Italian* borne to enjoy my laudes. At the last I haue found one aunswerable to my desire, *a Gentleman of great reuenewes, of a noble progenie, of honest behauiour, of comly personage,* borne and brought vp in *Naples,* Philautus (thy friend as I gesse) thy husband *Lucilla* if thou lyke it, neither canst thou dislyke him, who wanteth nothing that should cause thy liking, neither hath any thing that should breede thy loathing.

Ferardo says, '*mine only care hath been hitherto to match thee.* At last *I have found* one answerable to my desire, *a gentleman of great revenues,* of a *noble progeny,* of honest behaviour, of comely personage;' and Capulet says, '*my care hath been to have her* match'd and *having* now *provided a gentleman of noble parentage* of fair demesnes;' and the reader will see that Ferardo's description of Philautus closely resembles Capulet's description of Paris; that Ferardo had concluded with Philautus the marriage should immediately be consummated:—

> *La. Cap.* I will, and know her mind early to-morrow;
> To-night she is mew'd up to her heaviness.
> *Cap.* Sir Paris, I will make a desperate tender
> Of my child's love: I think she will be ruled
> In all respects by me; nay, more, I doubt it not.

Wife, go you to her ere you go to bed;
Acquaint her here of my son Paris' love;
And bid her, mark you me, on Wednesday next—
But, soft! what day is this?

   Par.   Monday, my lord.

   Cap. Monday! ha, ha! Well, Wednesday is too
     soon,
O' Thursday let it be: o' Thursday, tell her,
She shall be married to this noble earl.
Will you be ready? do you like this haste?
We'll keep no great ado,—a friend or two;
For, hark you, Tybalt being slain so late,
It may be thought we held him carelessly,
Being our kinsman, if we revel much:
Therefore we'll have some half a dozen friends,
And there an end. But what say you to Thursday?

   Par. My lord, I would that Thursday were tomorrow.

               Romeo and Juliet, Act iii. Scene 4.

and that Capulet and Paris had agreed that the marriage should be consummated on Thursday, Paris wishing that Thursday were to-morrow.

   Cap. How now, how now, chop-logic! What is
     this?
' Proud,' and ' I thank you,' and ' I thank you not:'
And yet ' not proud,' mistress minion, you,
Thank me no thankings, nor proud me no prouds,

But fettle your fine joints 'gainst Thursday next,
To go with Paris to Saint Peter's Church,
Or I will drag thee on a hurdle thither.
Out, you green-sickness *carrion!* out, you baggage!
You tallow-face!
    La. Cap.   Fie, fie! what, are you mad?
    Jul. Good father, I beseech you on my knees,
Hear me with patience, but to speak a word.
        Romeo and Juliet, Act iii. Scene 5.

I know what iarres, what ielousie, what strife, what stormes ensue, where the match is made rather by the compulsion of the parents, then by the consent of the parties: neither doe I like thee the lesse in that thou lykest *Philautus* so little, neither can *Philautus* loue thee ye worse in that thou louest thy selfe so well, wishing rather to stande to thy chaunce then to the choyce of any other. But this grieueth me most, that thou art almost vowed to the vayne order of the vestal virgins, dispising, or at the least not desiring, the sacred bandes of *Iuno,* hir bedde. If thy mother had bene of that minde when she was a mayden, thou haddest not nowe bene borne, to be of this minde to be a virgin. Way with thy selfe, what slender profit they bring to the common wealth, what slight pleasure to themselues, what great griefe to their parents, which ioy most in their offspring, and desire most to enioy the noble and blessed name of a graundfather. Thou knowest that the tallest Ash is cut down for fuell, bicause it beareth no good fruite: that the Cow that giues no milke is brought to the slaughter: that the Drone that gathereth no Honny is contemned: that the woman that maketh hir selfe barren by not marrying is accompted amonge the Grecian Ladyes worse then a *carryon*, as *Homer* reporteth.

La. Cap. Find thou the means, and I'll find such
    a man.
But now I'll tell thee joyful tidings, girl.
    Jul. And joy comes well in such a needy time:
What are they, I beseech your ladyship?
    La. Cap. Well, well, thou hast a careful father,
    child:
One who, to put thee from thy heaviness,
Hath sorted out a sudden day of joy,
That thou expect'st not nor I look'd not for.
    Jul. Madam, in happy time, what day is that?
    La. Cap. Marry, my child, early next Thursday
    morn,
The gallant, young and noble gentleman,
The County Paris, at Saint Peter's Church,
Shall happily make thee there a joyful bride.
    Jul. Now, by Saint Peter's Church and Peter
    too,
He shall not make me there a joyful bride.
I wonder at this haste: *that I must wed*
Ere he, that should be husband, comes to woo.
I pray you, tell my lord and father, madam,
I will not marry yet; and, when I do, I swear,
It shall be Romeo, whom you know I hate,
Rather than Paris. These are news indeed!
        Romeo and Juliet, Act iii. Scene 5.

Although *Philautus* thinke himselfe of vertue sufficient to winne his louer, yet shall he not obteine *Lucilla*. I cannot but smyle to heare yat a maryage should be solemnized, where neuer was any mention of assuring, and *that the wooing should be a daye after the wedding.*

Juliet wonders that she must wed ere he that should be her husband comes to woo, and Lucilla cannot but smile to hear that the wooing should be a day after the wedding.

Capulet wishes his daughter Juliet to marry Paris, Ferardo wishes his daughter Lucilla to marry Philautus; but Juliet loves Romeo, and Lucilla Euphues; and because Juliet and Lucilla seem reluctant to marry, the word *carrion* is applied to them. Juliet beseeches her father on her knees to hear her with patience, and Lucilla says to Ferardo—

My duetie therefore euer reserued, I here *on my knees* forsweare *Philautus* for my husband, although I accept him for my friend, and seeing I shal hardly be induced euer to match with any, I besech you if by your fatherly loue I shall be compelled, that I may match with such a one as both I may loue and you may lyke.

The reader may see other points of resemblance in these passages which I have not mentioned.

Cam.   There is a sickness
Which puts some of us in distemper, but
I cannot name the disease; and it is caught
Of you that yet are well.
   Pol.   How! caught of me!
Make me not *sighted like the basilisk:*
I have look'd on thousands, who have sped the
   better
By my regard, but kill'd none so.
              Winter's Tale, Act i. Scene 2.

We shunne the place of pestilence for feare of infection, the eyes of *Cathritiuss* bicause of diseases, the *sight of the Basilisk* for dreade of death, and shall wee not eschewe the companie of them that may entrappe vs in loue, which is more bitter then any distruction?

Fool. Canst tell how an oyster makes his shell?
Lear. No.
Fool. Nor I neither; but I can tell why *a snail has a house.*
Lear. Why?
Fool. Why, *to put his head in;* not to give it away to his daughters, and leave his horns without a case.
              Lear, Act i. Scene 5.

And seeing I cannot by reason restraine your

importunate suite, I will by rygour done on my selfe cause you to refraine the meanes. I would to God *Ferardo* were in this point lyke to *Lysander*, which woulde not suffer his daughters to weare gorgeous apparell, saying, it would rather make them common then comely. I would it were in *Naples* a lawe, which was a custome in *Aegypt*, that women should alwayes goe bare foote, to the intent they might keepe themselues alwayes at home, that they shold be euer like to *the Snaile, which hath euer his house on his head.*

King Richard. O, no! the apprehension of the
    good
Gives but the greater feeling to the worse:
Fell sorrow's tooth doth never rankle more
Than when he bites, but *lanceth* not the *sore*.
                    Richard II., Act i. Scene 3.

I had not thought to haue vsed so sower words, but where a wande cannot rule the horse, a spurre must. When gentle medicines haue no force to purge, wee must vse bitter potions: and where the *sore* is neither to be dissolued by plaister nor to be broken, it is requisite it should be *launced*.

Gremio. Sirrah, young gamester, your father
    were a fool
To give thee all, and in his waning age
Set foot under thy table: tut, a toy!
An old Italian fox is not so kind, my boy.   [*Exit.*

Tra. A vengeance on your crafty withered hide! Yet I have faced it *with a card of ten.*
Taming the Shrew, Act ii. Scene 1.

Is thy *cooling Carde* of this propertie, to quench fyre in others, and to kindle flames in thee? or is it a whetstone to make thee sharpe and vs blunt, or a sword to cut wounds in me and cure them in *Euphues*? Why didst thou write that agaynst them thou neuer thoughtest, or if thou diddest it, why doest thou not follow it? But it is lawfull for the Phisition to surfet, for the shepheard to wander, for *Euphues* to prescribe what he will, and do what he lyst.

The sick patient must keepe a straight diet, the silly sheepe a narrow folde, poore *Philautus* must beleeue *Euphues,* and all louers (he onelye excepted) are *cooled with a carde of tenne,* or rather fooled with a vaine toy.

Suf. Fond man, remember that thou hast a wife: Then how can Margaret be thy paramour?
Mar. I were best to leave him, for he will not hear.
Suf. There all is marr'd; there lies *a cooling card.*
1 *Henry VI.,* Act v. Scene 3.

Ah, fond *Euphues,* my deere friend, but a simple foole if thou beleeue now my *cooling Carde,* and an obstinate foole if thou do not recant it. But it may be thou layest that Carde for ye eleuation of *Naples* like an Astronomer. If it wer so I forgiue thee, for I must beleeue thee, if for the whole world.

. . . .

First let thy apparell be but meane, neyther too braue to shew thy pride, nor too base to betray thy pouertie; be as careful to keepe thy mouth from wine as thy fingers from fyre. Wine is the glasse of the minde, and the onely sauce that *Bacchus* gaue *Ceres* when he fell in loue; be not daintie mouthed, a fine taste noteth the fond appetites, that *Venus* sayde hir *Adonis* to haue, who seing him to take chiefest delight in costlie cates, smyling sayd this. I am glad that my *Adonis* hath a sweete tooth in his head, and who knoweth not what followeth. But I will not wade too farre, seeing heeretofore as wel in my *cooling card*, as at diuers other times, I haue giuen thee a caueat, in this vanity of loue to haue a care: and yet me thinketh the more I warne thee, the lesse I dare trust thee, for I know not how it commeth to passe, that euery minute I am troubled in minde about thee.

Lear. O me, my heart, my rising heart! but, down!

Fool. Cry to it, nuncle, as the *cockney* did to the eels when she put 'em i' the paste alive; she knapped 'em o' the coxcombs with a stick, and cried 'Down, *wantons*, down!' 'Twas her brother that, in pure kindness to his horse, buttered his hay.

Lear, Act ii. Scene 4.

Bast.   O inglorious league!
Shall we, upon the footing of our land,
Send fair-play orders and make compromise,
Insinuation, parley and base truce
To arms invasive? shall a beardless boy,
A *cockered* silken *wanton,* brave our fields,
And flesh his spirit in a warlike soil,
Mocking the air with colours idly spread,
And find no check?
                    King John, Act iv. Scene 1.

How dissolute haue I bene in striuing against good counsaile! how resolute in standing in mine own conceipt! how forward to wickednesse, how frowarde to wisdome! how *wantonne* with too much *cockering*! how wayward in hearing correction!

. . . .

I am nowe enforced to remember my mothers death, who I thinke was a Prophetesse in hir life, for oftentimes she woulde saye that thou haddest more beautie then was conuenient for one that shoulde bee honest, and more *cockering* then was meete for one that should be a Matrone.

. . . .

Nature will not permit me to disherit my daughter, and yet it would suffer thee to dishonour thy father. Affection causeth me to wish thy lyfe, and shall it entice thee to procure my death? It is mine onely comfort to see thee flourish in thy youth, and is it thine to see me fade in mine age? to conclude, I desire to liue to see thee prosper, and thou to see me perish. But why cast I the effecte of this vnnaturalnesse in thy teeth, seeing I my selfe was the cause? I made thee a *wanton*, and thou hast made me a foole: I brought thee vp like a *cockney*, and thou hast handled me like a cockescombe.

. . . .

As thy byrth doth shewe the expresse and liuely Image of gentle bloud, so thy bringing vp seemeth to mee to bee a great blotte to the lynage of so noble a brute, so that I am enforced to think that either thou diddest want one to giue thee good instructions, or that thy parents made thee a *wanton* with too much *cockering*: eyther they were too foolish in vsing no discipline, or thou too froward in reiecting their doctrine; either they willing to haue thee idle, or thou wilful to be il employed.

Laertes. He may not, as unvalu'd persons do,
Carve for himself; for on his choice depends
The safety and hea'th of the whole state.
Hamlet, Act i. Scene 3.

In meates, I loue to *carue* where I like, and in marriage shall I be *carued* where I lyke not? I had as liefe an other should take measure by his back of my apparell, as appoint what wife I shal haue, by his minde.

Macbeth. [*Aside*] Glamis, and thane of Cawdor!
The greatest is behind.
Macbeth, Act i. Scene 1.

Nowe when children shall by wisdome and vse refrayne from ouer-much tatling, let them also be admonished that when they shall speake, they speake nothing but truth: to lye is a vice most detestable, not to be suffered in a slaue, much lesse in a sonne. But *the greatest thing is yet behinde,* whether that those are to bee admytted as cockemates with children which loue them entirely, or whether they be to be banished from them.

Hero. Why, you speak truth. I never yet saw man,
How wise, how noble, young, how rarely featured,
But she would spell him backward: if fair-faced,
She would swear the gentleman should be her sister;
If black, why, Nature, drawing of an antique,
Made a foul blot; *if tall, a lance* ill-headed.
If low, an agate very vilely cut;
If speaking, why, a vane blown with all winds;
If silent, why, a block moved with none.
So turns she every man the wrong side out
And never gives to truth and virtue that
Which simpleness and merit purchaseth.
Much Ado about Nothing, Act iii. Scene 1.

Hero's account of Beatrice's method of spelling men backward was probably founded on the following passages in Euphues:—

Doe you not knowe the nature of women, which is grounded onely vpon extremities? Doe they thinke any man to delyght in them, vnlesse he doate on them? Any to be zealous except they bee iealous? Any to be feruent in case he be not furious? If he be cleanelye, then terme they him proude, if meane in apparell a slouen, *if talle a lungis, if short, a dwarfe,* if bolde, blunt: if shamefast, a cowarde: insomuch as they haue neither meane in their frumps, nor measure in their folly. But at the first the Oxe weyldeth not the yoke, nor the Colt the snaffle, nor the louer good counsel, yet time causeth the one to bend his neck, the other to open his mouth, and shoulde enforce the thirde to yeelde his right to reason. Laye before thine eyes the slightes and deceits of thy Lady, hir snatching in iest and keeping in earnest, hir periury, hir impietie, the countenance she sheweth to thee of course, the love she beareth to others of zeale, hir open malice, hir dissembled mischiefe.

O I woulde in repeating their vices thou couldest be as eloquent as in remembring them thou oughtest to bee penitent: be she neuer so comely call hir counterfaite, bee she neuer so straight thinke hir crooked. And wrest all partes of hir body to the worst, be she neuer so worthy. If shee be well sette, then call hir a Bosse; if *slender*, a *Hasill twygge*; if *Nutbrowne*, as blacke as a coale; if well couloured, a paynted wall; if shee bee pleasaunt, then is shee a wanton; if *sullenne*, a clowne; if honest, then is shee *coye*; if impudent, a harlot.

Kath. I chafe you, if I tarry: let me go,
Pet. No, not a whit: I find you passing gentle.
'Twas told me you were rough, and *coy* and *sullen*,
And now I find report a very liar;
For thou art pleasant, gamesome, passing courteous,
But slow in speech, yet sweet as spring-time flowers;
Thou canst not frown, thou canst not look askance,
Nor bite the lip, as angry wenches will,
Nor hast thou pleasure to be cross in talk,
But thou with mildness entertain'st thy wooers,
With gentle conference, soft and affable.
Why does the world report that Kate doth limp?
O slanderous world! Kate, like the *hazel-twig*,
Is straight and *slender*, and as *brown* in hue
As hazel-nuts, and sweeter than the kernels.
O, let me see thee walk: thou dost not halt.
Taming the Shrew, Act ii. Scene 1.

Come, thou monarch of the vine,
Plumpy Bacchus with *pink eyne!*
Antony and Cleopatra, Act ii. Scene 7.

Luc. Nay, now you are too flat
And mar the concord with too harsh a *descant*:
There wanteth but a mean to fill your song.
  Two Gentlemen of Verona, Act i. Scene 2.

Search euery vaine and sinewe of their disposition; if she haue no sight in *descante*, desire hir to chaunt it; if no cunning to daunce, request hir to trippe it; if no skill in musicke, profer hir the Lute; if an ill gate, then walke with hir; if rude in speach, talke with hir; if she be gagge toothed, tell her some merry iest, to make hir laughe; if *pinke eyed*, some dolefull Historye to cause hir weepe; in the one hir grinning will shew hir deformed, in the other hir whyning like a Pigge halfe rosted.

Petruchio. Faith, sirrah, an you'll not knock, I'll
  ring it;
I'll try how you can *sol, fa*, and sing it.
  Taming the Shrew, Act i. Scene 2.

The friendship betweene man and man as it is common so it is of course; betweene man and woman, as it is seldome so is it sincere, the one proceedeth of the similitude of manners, the other of ye sincerity of the heart: if thou haddest learned the first point of hauking, thou wouldst haue learned to haue held fast, or the first noat of *Descant*, thou wouldest haue kept thy *Sol. Fa.* to thy selfe.

Jul. What devil art thou, that dost torment me
    thus?
This torture should be roar'd in dismal hell.
Hath Romeo slain himself? say thou but 'I,'
And that bare vowel 'I' shall poison more
Than the death-darting eye of cockatrice;
I am not I, if there be such an I;
Or those eyes shut, that make thee answer 'I.'
If he be slain, say 'I'; or if not, no:
Brief sounds determine of my weal or woe.
        Romeo and Juliet, Act iii. Scene 2.

Shakespeare in this passage uses 'I' for ay. He may allude to some passages in Euphues like the following:—

Thou weepest for the death of thy daughter, and *I* laugh at the folly of the father, for greater vanitie is there in the minde of the mourner then bitternesse in the death of the deceased. But shee was amiable, but yet sinful, but she was young and might haue liued, but she was mortall and must haue dyed. *I* but hir youth made thee often merry, *I* but thine age shold once make thee wise. *I* but her greene yeares wer vnfit for death, *I* but thy hoary haires should dispyse life.

  .   .   .   .

If *Lucilla* be so proud to disdayne poore *Euphues*, woulde *Euphues* were so happye to denye *Lucilla* ; or if *Lucilla* be so *mortyfied* to lyue without loue, woulde *Euphues* were so fortunate to lyue in hate.

I but my colde welcome foretelleth my cold suit,
I but hir priuie glaunces signifie some good
Fortune.

. . . .

But this I conclude, that to barre one that is in
loue of the companye of his lady maketh him rather
madde then *mortified*, for him to refraine that neuer
knewe loue, is eyther to suspect him of folly without cause, or the next way for him to fall into folly
when he knoweth the cause.

. . . .

Besides this thy comly grace, thy rare qualyties,
thy exquisite perfection, were able to moue a minde
halfe *mortified* to transgresse the bonds of maidenly
modestie. But god shield *Lucilla*, that thou
shouldest be so carelesse of thine honour, as to commit the state thercoff to a straunger. Learne thou
by me *Euphues* to dispise things that be amiable,
to foregoe delightfull practises; beleeue mee it is
pietie to absteine from pleasure.

Dumain. My loving lord, Dumain is *mortified.*
The grosser manner of this world's delights
He throws upon the gross world's baser slaves.
   Love's Labour's Lost, Act i. Scene 1.

O infortunate *Philautus,* born in the wane of the
Moone, and as lykely to obtain thy wish as
the Wolfe is to catch the Moone. But why
goe I about to quench fire with a sword, or with
affection to *mortifie* my loue?

. . . .

G

I meane so to *mortifie* my selfe, that in steede of silkes, I wil weare sackcloth: for Owches and Bracelletes, Leere and Caddys: for the Lute, vse the Distaffe: for the Penne, the needle: for louers Sonettes, Dauids Psalmes.

. . . . . .

Mortifie therefore thy affections, and force not Nature against Nature to striue in vaine. Goe into the Contrey, looke to thy groundes, yoke thine Oxen, follow the Plough, graft thy trees, beholde thy cattell, and deuise with thy selfe, howe the encrease of them may encrease thy profite. In *Autumne* pull thine apples, in Summer ply thy haruest, in the Springe timme thy Gardens, in the Winter thy woodes, and thus beginninge to delyght to be a good husband, thou shalt begin to detest to be in loue with an idle huswife, when profite shall beginne to fill thy purse with golde, then pleasure shall haue no force to defile thy minde with loue.

Sir Andrew. I sent thee sixpence for thy *leman;* hadst it?
Twelfth Night, Act ii. Scene 3.

Ford. Help to search my house this one time. If I find not what I seek, show no colour for my extremity; let me for ever be your table-sport; let them say of me, ' As jealous as Ford, that searched *a hollow walnut* for his wife's *leman.*' Satisfy me once more; once more search with me.
Merry Wives of Windsor, Act iv. Scene 2.

What shall I gaine if I obteine my purpose? nay rather what shal I loose in winning my pleasure? If my Lady yeeld to be my louer, is it not likely she will be an others *lemman?* and if she be a modest matrone, my labour is lost. This therefore remaineth, that either I must pine in cares or perish with curses.

Shakespeare may, in this passage, refer to the method adopted by lovers of sending letters to each other in a hollow pomegranate. (*See* page 5.)

Ant. He shall kill two of us, and men indeed: But that's no matter; let him kill one first; *Win me and wear me;* let him answer me.
    Much Ado About Nothing, Act v. Scene 1.

Thou must chuse a woeman as the Lapidarie doth a true Saphire, who when he seeth it to glister, couereth it with oyle, and then if it shine, he alloweth it, if not, hee breaketh it: So if thou fall in loue with one that is beautifull, cast some kynde of coulour in hir face, eyther as it were myslyinge hir behauiour, or hearing of hir lightnesse, and if then shee looke as fayre as before, wooe hir, *win hir, and weare hir.*

Titus. He doth me wrong to *feed me with delays.*
    Titus Andronicus, Act iv. Scene 3.

And bicause I wil not *feede you with delayes*, nor that you should comfort your selfe with tryall, take this for a flatte aunswere, that as yet I meane not to loue any, and if I doe, it is not you, and so I leaue you.

―――

Holofernes. He is too *picked*, too spruce, too affected.
Love's Labour's Lost, Act v. Scene 1.

And so it fareth with loue, in tymes past they vsed to wooe in plaine tearmes, now in *picked* sentences, and hee speedeth best, that speaketh wisest: euery one following the newest waye, which is not euer the neerest way: some going ouer the stile when the gate is open, and other keeping the right beaten path, when hee maye crosse ouer better by the fieldes. Euery one followeth his owne fancie, which maketh diuers leape shorte for want of good rysinge, and many shoote ouer for lacke of true ayme.

―――

Petruchio. O, you are novices! 'tis a world to see,
How tame, when men and women are alone,
A *meacock* wretch can make the curstest shrew.
Taming the Shrew, Act ii. Scene 1.

King Richard. A *milk-sop* one that never in his life
Felt so much cold as over shoes in snow?
Richard III., Act v Scene 3.

Ant. Content yourself. God knows I loved my
niece;
And she is dead, slandered to death by villains,
That dare as well answer a man indeed
As I dare take a serpent by the tongue:
Boys, apes, braggarts, Jacks, *milksops!*
Much Ado About Nothing, Act iv. Scene 1.

To what ende then shall I liue in loue, seeing alwayes it is a life more to be feared than death? for all my time wasted in sighes and worne in sobbes, for all my treasure spente on Iewells, and spylte in iolyte, what recompence shall I reape besides repentaunce? What other reward shall I haue then reproch? What other solace then endles shame? But happely thou wylt saye, if I refuse their curtesie, I shall be accompted a *Mecocke,* a *Milksop,* taunted and retaunted with check and checkmate, flowted and reflowted with intollerable glee.

Biron. This gallant *pins the wenches on his sleeve;*
Had he been Adam, he had tempted Eve.
Love's Labour's Lost, Act v. Scene 2.

Alas fond foole, art thou so *pinned to their sleeues* yat thou regardest more their babble than thine own blisse, more their frumpes then thine owne welfare? Wilt thou resemble the kinde Spaniel, which the more he is beaten the fonder he is, or the foolish Giesse, which wil neuer away?

Armado. My *love* is most immaculate *white and red.*
    Love's Labour's Lost, Act i. Scene 2.

If ther were such a Ladie in this company *Surius,* that should wincke with both eyes when you would haue hir see your amourous lookes, or be no blabbe of hir tongue, when you would haue aunswere of your questions, I can-not thinke, that eyther hir vertuous conditions, or hir *white and red* complection coulde moue you to *loue.*

King Richard.   I say again, give out
That Anne my wife is sick and like to die:
About it; for *it stands me much upon,*
To stop all hopes whose growth may damage me.
    Richard III., Act iv. Scene 2.

Fidus, it *standeth thee vppon* eyther to winne thy loue or to weane thy affections, which choyce is so hard, that thou canst not tel whether the victory wil be the greater in subduing thy selfe, or conquering hir.

Paris. And Jove forbid there should be done
  amongst us
Such things as might offend the weakest spleen
To fight for and maintain!
Else might the world *convince* of levity
As well my undertakings as your counsels.
   Troilus and Cressida, Act ii. Scene 2.

Father and friend (your age sheweth the one, your honestie the other) I am neither so suspitious to mistrust your good wil, nor so sottish to mislike your good counsayle, as I am therfore to thanke you for the first, so it *standes me vpon* to thinke better on the latter: I meane not to cauil with you, as one louing sophistrie: neither to controwle you, as one hauing superioritie, the one woulde bring my talke into the suspition of fraude, the other *conuince* me of folly.

'Stand upon,' signifying to interest or concern, is often used by Shakespeare. Convince has, in these passages, the same meaning as convict.

Biron. Advance your standards, and upon them, lords;
Pell-mell, down with them! but be first advised,
In conflict that you get the sun of them.
Long. Now to plain-dealing; lay these *glozes* by.
Love's Labour's Lost, Act iv. Scene 3.

You preach Heresie, quoth *Philautus*, and besides so repugnant to the text you haue taken, that I am more ready to pull thee out of thy Pulpit, than to beleeue thy *gloses*.

. . . .

Touching tryall, I am neither so foolish to desire thinges impossible, nor so frowarde to request yat which hath no ende. But wordes shall neuer make me beleeue without workes, least in following a faire *shadowe*, I loose the firme *substance*, and in one worde set downe the onely triall that a Ladie requireth of hir louer, it is this, that he performe as much as he sware, that euery oathe be a deede, euery *gloase* a gospell, promising nothing in his talke, that he perform not in his triall.

Pro. Madam, if your heart be so obdurate,
Vouchsafe me yet your picture for my love,
The picture that is hanging in your chamber;
To that I'll speak, so that I'll sigh and weep:
For since the *substance* of your perfect self
Is else devoted, I am but a *shadow;*
And to your shadow will I make true love.
   Jul. [*Aside*] If 'twere a *substance*, you would, sure,
      deceive it,
And make it but a *shadow*, as I am.
   Sil. I am very loath to be your idol, sir;
But since your falsehood shall become you well
To worship shadows and adore false shapes,
Send to me in the morning and I'll send it.
   Two Gentlemen of Verona, Act iv. Scene 2.

Liuia replyed: Sir, our country is ciuile, and our gentlewomen are curteous, but in *Naples* it is compted a iest, at euery word to say, In faith you are welcome. As she was yet talking, supper was set on the bord, then *Philautus* spake thus vnto *Lucilla*. Yet Gentlewoman, I was the bolder to bring my *shadow* with me (meaning *Euphues*), knowing that he should be the better welcome for my sake: vnto whom the Gentlewoman replyed: Sir, as I neuer when I saw you, thought that you came without your *shadow*, so now I cannot a lyttle meruaile to see you so ouershot in bringing a new *shadow* with you. *Euphues*, though he percieued hir coy nippe, seemed not to care for it, but taking hir by the hand said.

Faire Lady, seeing the shade doth often shield your beautie from the parching Sunne, I hope you will the better esteeme of the *shadow*, and by so much the lesse it ought to be offensiue, by how much the lesse it is able to offende you, and by so much the more you ought to lyke it, by how much the more you vse to lye in it.

Well Gentleman, aunswered *Lucilla*, in arguing of the *shadow*, we forgoe the *substaunce*: pleaseth it you therefore to sit downe to supper. And so they all sate downe, but *Euphues* fed of one dish, which euer stoode before him, the beautie of *Lucilla*.

Ulyss. May worthy Troilus be half *attach'd*
With that which here his passion doth express?
   Tro. Ay, Greek; and that shall be divulged
     well
In characters as red as Mars his heart
Inflamed with Venus: never did young man fancy
With so eternal and so fix'd a soul.
       Troilus and Cressida, Act v. Scene 2.

Rosalind. There is a man haunts the forest, that abuses our young plants with carving 'Rosalind' on their barks; hangs odes upon hawthorns and elegies on brambles, all, forsooth, deifying the name of Rosalind: if I could meet that *fancy*-monger, I would give him some good counsel, for he seems to have the *quotidian of love* upon him.
As You Like It, Act iii. Scene 2.

Juliet. O nature, what hadst thou to do in hell, When thou didst bower the spirit of a fiend In mortal paradise of such sweet flesh? Was ever book containing such vile matter So fairly bound? O, that *deceit should dwell In such a gorgeous palace!*
Romeo and Juliet, Act iii. Scene 2.

Doubtlesse if euer she hir selfe haue bene scorched with the flames of desire, she wil be redy to quench the coales with curtesie in an other: if euer she haue bene *attached of loue,* she will rescue him that is drenched in desire: if euer she haue ben taken with the feuer of *fancie,* she will help his ague, who by a *quotidian* fit is connerted into phrensie: neither can ther be vnder so *delycate a hue lodged deceipt,* neither in so beautiful a mould, a malicious minde.

And when thou comst thy tale to tell, Smooth not thy tongue with *filed talk.*
The Passionate Pilgrim.

Holofernes. His humour is lofty, his discourse peremptory, his *tongue filed.*
   Love's Labour's Lost, Act v. Scene 1.

Farewell therefore the fine and *filed* phrases of *Cicero,* the pleasaunt *Eligues* of *Ouid,* the depth and profound knowledge of *Aristotle.* Farewell Rhethoricke, farewell Philosophie, farewel al learning which is not sprong from the bowells of the holy Bible.

. . . .

O my *Euphues,* lyttle dost thou knowe the sodeyn sorrowe that I susteine for thy sweete sake : Whose wyt hath bewitched me, whose rare qualyties haue depryued me of myne olde qualytie, most curteous behauiour without curiositie, whose comely feature, wythout fault, whose *filed speach* without fraud, hath wrapped me in this misfortune.

Iago. These Moors are changeable in their wills; —fill thy purse with money :—the food that to him now is as luscious as locusts, shall be to him shortly as bitter as *coloquintida.*
   Othello, Act i. Scene 3.

Hamlet. So, oft it chances in particular men,
That for some *vicious mole* of nature in them,
As, in their birth—wherein they are not guilty,
Since nature cannot choose his origin—
By the o'ergrowth of some complexion,

Oft breaking down the pales and forts of reason,
Or by some habit that too much o'er-leavens
The form of plausive manners, that these men,
Carrying, I say, the stamp of *one defect*,
Being nature's livery, or fortune's star,—
Their virtues else—be they as pure as grace,
As infinite as man may undergo—
Shall in the general censure take corruption
From that particular fault: *the dram of eale*
Doth *all* the noble substance of a doubt
To his own scandal.
                                Hamlet, Act i. Scene 4.

Alas *Euphues* by how much the more I see the high clymbing of thy capacitie, by so much the more I feare thy fall. The fine Christall is sooner erased then the hard Marble: the greenest Beech, burneth faster then the dryest Oke: the fairest silke is soonest soyled: and the sweetest Wine, tourneth to the sharpest Vineger. The Pestilence doth most rifest infect the clearest complection, and the Caterpiller cleaueth vnto the ripest fruite: the most delycate witte is allured with small enticement vnto *vice*, and most subiect to yeelde vnto vanitie. If therefore thou doe but hearken to the *Syrenes*, thou wilt be enamoured: if thou haunt their houses and places, thou shalt be enchaunted. *One droppe of poyson infecteth the whole tunne of Wine:* one leafe of *Colloquintida*, marreth and spoyleth the whole pot of porredge: one yron *Mole*, defaceth the whole peece of Lawne.

Shakespeare says, that particular men, owing to some *vicious mole* of nature in them, or the stamp of *one defect,* shall in the general censure take corruption from this particular fault,—

The dram of eale
Doth *all* the noble substance of a doubt
To his own scandal.

And Lyly says, *one drop of poison* infecteth the *whole* tun of wine, *one iron mole* defaceth the whole piece of Lawne.

'Dram of eale' may be a misprint or abbreviation of 'dram of hellebore,' or 'elebore,' which old authors speak of as being very poisonous; for example, Stephen Gosson, in his 'Schoole of Abuse,' published in 1579, thus speaks of it:—' One dramme of Eleborus ransackes every vein.'

The commentators have given many drams to this passage, including 'dram of ease,' 'dram of base,' 'dram of ill,' 'dram of ale,' 'dram of lead,' 'dram of ail,' 'dram of evil,' 'drams of vile,' 'dram of calce,' 'dram of earth.'

Enter Apothecary.

Ap. Who calls so loud?
Rom. Come hither, man. I see that thou art
  poor:
Hold, there is forty ducats: let me have
A dram of *poison*, such soon-speeding gear
As will disperse itself through all the veins
That the life-weary taker may fall dead
And that the trunk may be discharged of breath
As violently as hasty powder fired
Doth hurry from the fatal cannon's womb.
  Romeo and Juliet, Act v. Scene 1.

Your humour is to be purged not by the *Apothecaries confections*, but by the following of good counsaile. You are in loue *Fidus?* Which if you couer in a close chest, will burne euery place before it burst the locke. For as we know by Phisick that *poyson wil disperse it selfe into euery veyne*, before it part the hart: so I haue heard by those yat in *loue* could say somwhat, that it maimeth euerye parte, before it kill the *Lyuer*.

Ford. Love my wife!
Pist. With *liver* burning hot.
  Merry Wives of Windsor, Act ii. Scene 1.

The idea of her life shall sweetly creep
Into his study of imagination,
And every lovely organ of her life
Shall come apparell'd in more precious habit,
More moving-delicate and full of life,

Into the eye and prospect of his soul,
Than when she lived indeed; then shall he mourn,
If ever *love* had interest in his *liver*,
And wish he had not so accused her,
No, though he thought his accusation true.
Much Ado About Nothing, Act iv. Scene 2.

Duke. There is no woman's sides
Can bide the beating of so strong a passion
As love doth give my heart; no woman's heart
So big, to hold so much; they lack retention.
Alas their *love* may be call'd appetite,
No motion of the *liver*, but the palate,
That suffer surfeit, cloyment and revolt.
Twelfth Night, Act ii. Scene 4.

For as the Hoppe, the poale beeing neuer so hye, groweth to the ende, or as the drye Beech kindled at the roote, neuer leaueth vntill it come to the toppe: or as *one droppe of poyson disperseth it selfe into euery vaine*, so affection hauing caught holde of my heart, and the sparkles of loue kindled my *Lyuer*, wyll sodeynelye, though secretly, flame vp into my heade, and spreade it selfe into euerye sinewe.

In these passages, Shakespeare and Lyly connect the word 'love' with the word 'liver,' said to be the seat of love.

King. The skipping king, he ambled up and down
With shallow jesters and rash *bavin* wits,
Soon kindled and soon burnt.
     1 *Henry IV.*, Act iii. Scene 2.

Yet will you commonly obiect this to such as serue you, and starue to winne your good wil, that hot loue is soone colde: that the *Bauin* though it burne bright, is but a blaze.

But it may be that as the sight of diuers colours, makes diuers beasts madde: so my presence doth driue thee into this melancholy. And seeing it is so, I will absent my selfe, hier an other lodging in *London*, and for a time giue my selfe to my booke, for I haue learned this by experience, though I be young, that *Bauins* be knowen by their bands, Lyons by their clawes, Cockes by their combes, enuious mindes by their manners.

Cas.   Brutus, bay not me;
I'll not endure it: you forget yourself,
To *hedge me in;* I am a soldier, I,
Older in practice, abler than yourself
To make conditions.
     Julius Cæsar, Act iv. Scene 3.

As husbandmen hedge in their trees, so should good schoolemasters with good manners *hedge in* the wit and disposition of the scholler, whereby the blossomes of learning may the sooner encrease to a budde.

THE EMPTY VESSEL MAKES THE GREATEST SOUND. 97

Talbot. A witch, by fear, not force, like Hannibal,
Drives back our troops and conquers as she lists:
So bees with *smoke* and doves with noisome stench
Are from their *hives* and houses *driven away.*
1 *Henry VI.*, Act i. Scene 5.

King. How fares our cousin Hamlet?
Ham. Excellent i' faith; of the *chameleon's* dish:
I eat the air, promise-crammed: you cannot feed capons so.
Hamlet, Act iii. Scene 2.

Boy. I did never know so full a voice issue from so empty a heart: but the saying is true, ' *The empty vessel makes the greatest sound.*'
Henry V., Act iv. Scene 4.

They that vse to steale Honny burne Hemlocke *to smoake the Bees from their hiues,* and it may bee, that to get some aduauntage of me, you haue vsed these smoakie arguments, thinking thereby to smother me with the conceipt of strong imagination. But as the *Camelion though he haue most guttes draweth least breath,* or as the Elder tree though hee bee fullest of pith, is farthest from strength: so though your resons seeme inwardly to your selfe somewhat substantiall, and your perswasions pithie in your owne conceipte, yet beeing well wayed without, they be shadows without substaunce, and weake without force. The bird *Taurus* hath a great voyce, but a smal body: the thunder a great

H

clap, yet but a lyttle stone: the *emptie vessell giueth a greater sound then the full barrell.*

The boy says, 'I did never know so *full a voice* issue from so *empty* a heart,' and Lyly, that 'the bird Taurus hath *a great voice,* but a small body;' and Lyly and Shakespeare both say, the empty vessel gives or makes the greatest sound.

Edm. Thou *nature,* art my *goddess;* to thy law My services are bound.
Lear, Act i. Scene 2.

Nature was had in such estimation and admiration among the Heathen people, that she was reputed for the onely *Goddesse* in heauen.

Ther. Why, he stalks up and down like a peacock,—a stride and a stand: ruminates like an hostess that hath no arithmetic but her brain to set down her reckoning: bites his lip with a politic regard, as who should say 'There were wit in this head, an 'twould out;' and so there is, but *it lies as coldly in him as fire in a flint,* which will not show without knocking.
Troilus and Cressida, Act iii. Scene 3.

But yet I am not so senceles altogether to reiect your seruice: which if I wer certeinly assured to proceede of a simple mind, it shold not receiue so simple a reward. And what greater tryall can I haue of thy simplicitie and truth, then thine owne request which desireth a triall. I, but *in the coldest flint there is hot fire*, the Bee that hath hunny in hir mouth, hath a sting in hir tayle.

Cost. Not so, sir; *under correction,* sir; I hope it
  is not so.
You cannot beg us, sir, I can assure you, sir; we
  know what we know:
I hope, sir, three times thrice, sir,—
  Biron. Is not nine.
  Cost. Under correction, sir, we know whereuntil
t doth amount.
Love's Labour's Lost, Act v. Scene 2.

Nowe where-as you sette downe, that loue commeth not from the eyes of the woeman, but from the glaunces of the man (*under correction* be it spoken) it is as farre from the trueth, as the head from the toe.

Mistris *Frauncis,* you resemble in your sayings the Painter *Tamantes,* in whose pictures there was euer more vnderstoode then painted: for with a *glose* you seeme to shadow yat, which in colours you will not shewe. It can-not be, my *violet,* that the faster I run after you, the farther I shoulde bee from you, vnlesse that eyther you haue wings tyed to your heeles, or I thornes thrust into mine.

H 2

Duch. Welcome, my son, *who* are the *violets* now
That strew the green lap of the new come spring?
Aum. Madam, I know not, nor I greatly care not:
God knows I had as lief be none as one.
York. Well, bear you well in this new spring of
  time,
Lest you be cropp'd before you come to prime.
Richard II., Act v. Scene 2.

I haue not forgotten one Mistres *Frauncis*, which the Ladye *Flauia* gaue thee for a *Violet*, and by thy description, though she be not equall with *Camilla*, yet is she fitter for *Philautus*. If thy humour be such that nothing can feede it but loue, cast thy minde on hir, conferre the impossibilytie thou hast to winne *Camilla*, with the lykelyhoode thou mayst haue to enioy thy *Violet*: and in this I will endeauour both my wit and my good will, so that nothing shall want in mee, that may work ease in thee. Thy *Violet* if she be honest, is worthy of thee, beautiful thou sayst she is, and therefore too worthy: Hoat fire is not onely quenched by ye cleere Fountaine, nor loue onely satisfied by the faire face. Therefore in this tell me thy minde, that either we may proceede in that matter, or seeke a newe medicine. *Philautus* thus replyed.

King. The harlot's cheek, beautied with plas-
  tering art,
Is not more ugly to the thing that helps it
Than is my deed to my most *painted word.*
Hamlet, Act iii. Scene 1.

Mrs. Page. 'Tis old, but true,—' Still swine eat all the *draff*.'
Merry Wives of Windsor, Act iv. Scene 2.

Falstaff. You would think that I had a hundred and fifty tattered prodigals, lately come from swine-keeping, from eating *draff* and husks.
1 *Henry IV.*, Act iv. Scene 2.

Draffe was mine errand, but drinke I would, my great curtesie was to excuse my greeuous tormentes: for I ceased not continuallye to courte my *violette*, whome I neuer found so coye as I thought, nor so curteous as I wished. At the last, thinkinge not to spend all my wooinge in signes, I fell to flatte sayinges, reuealing the bytter sweetes that I sustained, the ioy at hir presence, the grief at hir absence, with all speeches that a *Louer* myght frame: She not degenerating from the wyles of a woeman, seemed to accuse men of inconstancie, that the *painted wordes* were but winde, that feygned sighes were but sleyghtes, that all their loue was but to laugh, laying baites to catch the fish, that they meant agayne to throw into the ryuer, practisinge onelye cunninge to deceyue, not curtesie, to tell trueth, where-in she compared all Louers, to *Mizaldus* the Poet, which was so lyght that euery winde would blowe him awaye, vnlesse hee had lead tyed to his heeles, and to the fugitiue stone in *Cyzico*, which runneth away if it be not fastened to some post.

The Duchess asks Aumerle ' *who* are the

violets now that strew the green lap of the new come spring,' and I think she plays upon the word, using it in its ordinary sense, and also in the sense in which it is used in these passages in 'Euphues,' where it seems to signify a lover or sweetheart.

Philautus, if thy *Vyolet* seeme in the first moneth either to chide or chafe, thou must heare with out reply, and endure it with patience, for they that cannot suffer the wranglyngs of young marryed women, are not vnlyke vnto those, that tasting the grape to be sower before it be ripe, *leaue to* gather it when it is ripe, resemblyng them, that being stong with the Bee, forsake the Honny.

I cannot *leave to* love, and yet I do;
But there I *leave to* love where I should love.
  Two Gentlemen of Verona, Act ii. Scene 6.

 Hamlet. Could you on this fair mountain *leave to* feed, and batten on this moor?
     Hamlet, Act iii. Scene 4.

 Euery action hath his ende and then we *leaue to* sweat when we haue founde the sweete. The Ant though she toyle in Summer, yet in Winter shee *leueth to* trauaile.

 Pan. You have no judgment, niece: Helen herself swore th' other day, that Troilus, for a *brown favour*—for so 'tis, I must confess,—not brown neither,—

Cres. No, but brown.
Pan. 'Faith, to say truth, brown and not brown.
Cres. To say the truth, true and not true.
Pan. She praised his complexion above Paris.
Cres. Why, Paris hath colour enough.
Pan. So he has.
Cres. Then Troilus should have too much: if she praised him above, his complexion is higher than his; he having colour enough, and the other higher, is too flaming a praise for a good complexion. I had as lief Helen's golden tongue had commended Troilus for a copper nose.

Troilus and Cressida, Act i. Scene 2.

Bene. Why, i' faith, methinks she's *too low* for a high praise, *too brown* for a fair praise and too little or a great praise: only this *commendation* I can afford her, that were she other than she is, she were unhandsome; and being no other but as she is, I do not like her.

Much Ado About Nothing, Act i. Scene 1.

A noble man in *Sienna*, disposed to iest with a gentlewoman of meane birth, yet excellent qualities, between game and earnest gan thus to salute hir. I know not how I shold *commend* your beautie, because it is somwhat too *brown*, nor your stature being somwhat *too low*, and of your wit I can not iudge, no, quoth she, I beleeue you, for none can iudge of wit, but they that haue it, why then, quoth he, *doest thou thinke me a foole, thought is free* my Lord quoth she, I wil not take you at your word.'

Sir And. An you part so, mistress, I would I might never draw sword again. Fair lady, *do you think you have fools in hand?*
Mar. Sir, I have not you by the hand.
Sir And. Marry, but you shall have; and here's my hand.
Mar. Now, sir, '*thought is free:*' I pray you, bring your hand to the buttery-bar and let it drink.
Twelfth Night, Act i. Scene 3.

Benedict says, 'she's *too low* for a high praise, *too brown* for a fair praise, only this *commendation* I can afford her,' and Lyly says, 'I know not how I should *commend* your beauty, because it is somewhat *too brown,* nor your stature, being somewhat *too low.*' Sir Andrew says, 'Fair lady, do you think you have fools in hand?' and Maria says, 'Now, sir, thought is free;' and the words are similar in 'Euphues,' 'dost thou think me a fool ; thought is free.'

Suffolk. Smooth runs the water where the brook is
  deep:
And in his simple show he harbours treason.
The fox barks not when he would steal the lamb.
No, no, my sovereign; Gloucester is a man
Unsounded yet and full of deep deceit.
2 *Henry VI.,* Act iii. Scene 1.

I perceiue *Issida* that *where the streame runneth
smoothest the water is deepest,* and where the least
smoake is, there to be the greatest fire: and wher the
mildest countenaunce is, there to be the melan-
choliest conceits. I sweare to thee by the Gods,
and there she interrupted me againe, in this manner.
  Fidus the more you sweare, the lesse I beleeue
you, for that it is a practise in Loue, to haue as
little care of their owne oathes, as they haue of others
honors, imitating *Iupiter,* who neuer kept oath he
swore to *Iuno,* thinking it lawfull in loue to haue
as small regard of Religion, as he had of chastitie.

  Phi.   Have patience, sir,
And take your ring again; 'tis not yet won:
It may be probable she lost it; or
Who knows if one of her women, being corrupted,
Hath stol'n it from her?
  Post.   Very true;
And so, I hope, he came by't. Back my ring:
Render to me some corporal sign about her,
More evident than this; for this was stolen.
  Iach. By Jupiter, I had it from her arm.

> *Post.* Hark you, he swears; *by Jupiter he swears.*
> 'Tis true:—nay keep the ring—'tis true: I am sure
> She would not lose it: her attendants are
> All sworn and honourable:—they induced to steal it!
> 				*Cymbeline,* Act ii. Scene 4.

Iachimo wished Posthumus to believe his account of Imogen's infidelity, and he swears by Jupiter, who 'thought it lawful in love to have as small regard of religion as he had of chastity;' and Posthumus says, 'by Jupiter he swears. 'Tis true,'—seeming to connect the immorality of Jupiter with the conduct of Iachimo, and the alleged frailty of Imogen.

Much of the philosophy and various knowledge, and many of the fine thoughts and touches of nature in Shakespeare, I see in the works of old authors who wrote before his time. Even many of the quibbles and bad puns, for using which he has been censured, are not his own.

Lyly's works must have been well known to the educated frequenters of the Globe, and I think that Shakespeare often appealed to the knowledge of his audiences, who would easily recognise the allusions to 'Euphues,' and I can well fancy with what admiration and applause they would greet the first appearance of the magnificent structures, which his splendid genius had raised from such meagre materials.

THE END.

www.ingramcontent.com/pod-product-compliance
Lightning Source LLC
Chambersburg PA
CBHW021945160426
43195CB00011B/1227